Eerie OKLAHOMA

Eerie
OKLAHOMA

Heather Woodward

Illustrations by Rebecca Lindsey
Foreword by Stephanie Carrell

THE
History
PRESS

Published by The History Press
Charleston, SC
www.historypress.com

First published 2022

Manufactured in the United States

ISBN 9781467151917

Library of Congress Control Number: 2022936212

Notice: The information in this book is true and complete to the best of our knowledge. It is offered without guarantee on the part of the author or The History Press. The author and The History Press disclaim all liability in connection with the use of this book.

This book is dedicated to the loudest, grouchiest and fiercest little chihuahua: Peanut. You were the best traveling buddy and paranormal sidekick. I hope they have chewing bones on the other side of the rainbow bridge.
You will forever be missed.

CONTENTS

Foreword, by Stephanie Carrell   9
Acknowledgements   13
Introduction   15
    A Brief Introduction of the Sooner State   16
    Trail of Tears   17
    The Tulsa Massacre   18
    The Oklahoma City Bombings   20
    The Survivor Tree   23

Part I. Legends and Lore   25
1. The Yunwi Tsunsdi   27
2. The Stikini (Owl Man)   30
3. The Legend of John Wilkes Booth   33
4. The Center of the Universe   40
5. Shaman Portal   43
6. The Spook Light   45

Part II. Ghosts and Ghouls   49
7. Crybaby Bridge   51
8. Dead Woman's Crossing   53
9. Hex House   56
10. Stone Lion Inn   64
11. Northeastern State University Seminary Hall   70
12. Overholser Mansion   73

Part III. Creepy Cryptids   75
13. Bigfoot   77
14. The Green Hill Monster   80
15. The Deer Woman (The Deer Lady)   83
16. The Oklahoma Octopus   86

Part IV. Murder and Mystery   91
17. The Hanging Tree   93
18. Joan Gay Croft   95
19. The Giggling Granny   101
20. The Lawton Serial Killer   105
21. The Camp Scott Girl Scout Murders   112

Conclusion   127
Bibliography   129
Contributors   137
About the Author   139

FOREWORD

In early 2015, in the middle of my spiritual awakening, I stumbled on a Facebook post by a business coach who was promoting one of her clients. Intrigued by the promise of expanding my psychic abilities and the enticement of a pay-what-you-want offer, I clicked and paid ten or fifteen dollars to a random person for a program I knew nothing about.

Seven years later, that initial investment has paid me back in ways I could never have imagined. Not only have my psychic abilities grown exponentially, but I have also met a group of amazingly powerful women, gone on insane adventures I still cannot believe happened and made a wonderful friend.

When Heather approached me with this book, I did not hesitate to help investigate and share my knowledge of the state. Growing up in Oklahoma has had its pros and cons. I have traveled the majority of the United States, and so far, no other place has called me away. The one thing I am asked most when I say I'm from Oklahoma is, "Have you ever been in a tornado?" Honestly, no, I have not been in a tornado. Other than wall clouds in the distance, I have not even seen one in person. I may not have experienced a tornado firsthand, but I have lived in the aftermath of many.

The majority of tornadoes that develop are weak, cause minimal damage and tend to land in open fields and the countryside. The devastating EF-5 tornadoes that make headlines are rare, usually with several years if not decades between them.

I grew up in Woodward, a small town in Northwest Oklahoma with a surprisingly significant history. General Custer traveled through the area to set up the nearby Fort Supply during the Indian Wars, Temple Houston's historic "Soiled Dove Plea" echoed through the makeshift courtroom of the opera house and, in 1947, the town experienced the deadliest tornado in the state's history.

Hearing stories of the '47 tornado was part of life growing up. Our occasional trips to the Plains Indians and Pioneers Museum put me up close and personal with the devastation. The images soaked into my brain as a small child. The debris was cleared and the town rebuilt, but the impact of that day never left.

Forty-five years later, Woodward experienced another weather anomaly. On April 9, 1992, I was living in Oklahoma City with my mom. That evening, I picked up the phone and dialed my grandma's number. The phone lines were busy. I could not get through, even after multiple attempts. Later, we learned that a storm system had developed seven tornadoes that were encircling the town. Due to the slow-moving system, the tornadoes appeared to be staying in place before dissipating approximately ninety minutes later.

One year later, I saw my classmates and familiar homes and buildings in an episode of *Unsolved Mysteries*. Living back in Woodward, I remember the school bus having to detour while they filmed at the "Old Hospital." The tornado had crept into our lives once again.

To commemorate the fiftieth anniversary of the storm in 1997, the town built a time capsule in the side of the new middle school cafeteria. A handful of my classmates and I wrote essays that are enclosed and will be read when it is opened in 2047.

April 7, 2022, marks the semisesquicentennial of that deadly tornado and the mysterious story of a young girl who has sparked the curiosity of the world.

Psychically, there is something odd about the area. It feels as if the energy is pooling in the heart of the town. I am not sure if it is due to the land's topography and minerals in the soil, a crossing of highways, residual energy from the tornado or a combination of them all. There is a palpable difference that can be felt about ten miles outside of town and intensifies as you come nearer.

I really never noticed this until I moved away and had kids. There is a particular point on the road where you start to get antsy and fidgety. Usually, this is where my kids start arguing or fighting with each other. It makes those last few miles of the trip extremely intense at times.

I believe this energy, whatever it is from, is partially responsible for the high drug use, mental health problems and slew of other unsettling incidents that have occurred there over the years. Unfortunately, this is not unique to the small corner of Oklahoma where I was raised. There are several locations throughout the state with this type of intense energy. Many have chilling stories of their own.

On the pages of this book, you will discover tales from across the state of mystery, murder and magical creatures. This is not the state portrayed in the musical. This is *Eerie Oklahoma*.

—Stephanie Carrell

ACKNOWLEDGEMENTS

Thank you to Buck Mulle for letting me drag you to a bunch of weird locations in Oklahoma and for putting up with my long hours of writing.

Thank you to Rebecca Lindsey for being the most awesome illustrator ever!

Extra special thanks to Stephanie Carrell for going above and beyond with your help, guidance and devoted support. May Brigid and Elen smile upon you!

Thank you to my son and my mom for being super supportive and always being there for me.

INTRODUCTION

Oklahoma is one of those overlooked states that has a lot of interesting legends, lore and unexplained phenomena but does not get credit for it. It is nestled on top of its larger, more obnoxious brother state, Texas, which seems to always be in the news for its shenanigans. I'm mean, how many times has Texas threatened to secede the United States or put some random law into effect that angers the rest of the country?

Though smaller and quieter, Oklahoma is mighty when it comes to the unexplained and the macabre. Much of the folklore of the Sooner State comes from the lush history of the Native Americans who were transplanted here after the Trail of Tears. However, there are tales from the days of the Confederacy and beyond that create an impression on its lore.

There's a story about a corpse that traveled the world so that patrons could gawk at the man who allegedly killed the president of the United States. His real identity is unknown to this day, but the legend says he's a mastermind of being elusive and cheating death more than once.

There are plenty of strange sightings in Oklahoma, from skunk ape to bigfoot to the green hill monster. The heavily wooded terrain hides all kinds of undetermined cryptid wildlife that locals have witnessed with fear and trepidation. There are festivals to commemorate and validate those who have experienced the unknown and still live to tell their tales.

Let's not forget the one and only lake monster in Oklahoma. It's reddish tentacles lure men to unfortunate fates. Part–Native American lore and part–pop culture fanfare, the creature stalks not one but three lakes in the

Sooner State. With drowning rates skyrocketing nearly 40 percent in the last ten years, it's not surprising the creature has created a foothold in our imaginations. Is it man's folly, or it could be something sinister pulling people into the abyss?

Oklahoma is not without its true crime cases and unsolved murders. Interstates 40 and 44 run through the state, bringing with them a slew of dumped bodies on the side of road, unrecognizable women who can't be identified because of unpredictable weather and watery graves that wash away evidence are scooped up by officials.

Then there's the case that people still whisper about at parties, even though it's over forty years old. Three young girls were murdered at a Girl Scout camp in a crowded area in plain sight. There were twenty-eight tents around them, and no one saw a thing. A man was apprehended, but he swore he didn't do it and a jury believed him. Justice never prevailed, and the townsfolk in the area still wonder what really happened.

Oklahoma likes to keep its secrets. It likes to keep its lore quiet. But if you do some digging and you ask the right questions, the story will unfold—just maybe not in the way you thought it would.

So, get a snack, have a drink and get comfortable. I'm sharing with you what I have found while living in the Sooner State. I'll divulge some mysteries and give you the details. And if you want, you can find these strange places and experience them yourself. Just don't get mad at me if you end up sucked into a portal and must live the rest of your life in another dimension.

A Brief History of the Sooner State

Oklahoma, east of the Panhandle, was acquired as part of the Louisiana Purchase in 1803. The rest of Oklahoma became part of the state after the land deals of the Mexican-American War.

A large portion of Oklahoma was set aside for Indian Territory and did not officially open for settlement until April 1889. Those who wanted to acquire land in Oklahoma settled on the state border, waiting the official word from President Benjamin Harrison. They were called "Boomers," and they followed the policies of land acquisition.

However, there were those who snuck across the border and set claim to land illegally. They were called "Sooners" and had a bad reputation. Other settlers considered them liars and thieves.

By the early 1900s, the name *Sooner* became an affectionate slang term for the people living in Oklahoma because it had an air of rebellion and freedom associated with the Wild West. In 1908, the Oklahoma State University teams used the term "Sooners" as their name. By the 1920s, the state was affectionately nicked name the "Sooner Sate," and it has stuck to this day.

Trail of Tears

The Trail of Tears was a ten-year forced relocation of the Native American tribes in the southeast region of the United States. Approximately 100,000 Indigenous people from the Muscogee, Cherokee, Seminole, Chickasaw and Choctaw tribes were forcibly removed from their ancestral homes and pushed into designated territories west of the Mississippi River. According to tribal and military records, around 15,000 Native Americans perished from starvation, disease and exposure during the journey

The routes spanned 5,045 miles and nine states, including Alabama, Arkansas, Georgia, Illinois, Kentucky, Missouri, North Carolina, Oklahoma and Tennessee. Most routes went over land, but there was one water route that required boats to travel down riverways. The evacuation started with

An overview of the Tulsa Race Riot in 1921. *From Wikimedia Commons.*

federal troops pushing people out of their homes and then traveling by foot for over thousands of miles for several weeks with extraordinarily little food and provisions.

The Trail of Tears Forced Relocation Act ended in March 1893. Its last stop was Tahlequah, Oklahoma, which is now the capital of the Cherokee Nation.

The Cherokee Nation is a sovereign tribal government set up by Native American tribes after the Indian Removal Act. On September 6, 1893, the new government adopted its own constitution. Today, the Cherokee Nation has about 390,000 members throughout the United States. More than 141,000 tribal members live within the nation's reservation boundaries in northeastern Oklahoma. The government supplies healthcare and human services, education programs, housing and much more.

You can visit the Trail of Tears National Historic Trail, which traces the route used to reach the city. At the Heritage Center, there are sixteen thousand handmade beads commemorating the lives of each person who made the trip to Tahlequah, Oklahoma.

Go to the following website to plan your trip to the Historic Park and the Heritage Center: https://www.nps.gov/trte/planyourvisit/index.htm.

The Tulsa Massacre

Said to be the single worst racially driven event in American history, the Tulsa Massacre spanned eighteen hours and killed between fifty and three hundred people. The incident took place between May 31 and June 1, 1921, when a Black shoeshiner, Dick Rowland, was accused of raping a seventeen-year-old woman named Sarah Page who was an elevator operator at the Drexel building.

Rowland was taken into custody, and rumors quickly spread that he was going to be hanged for the crime. An inflammatory article in the *Tulsa Tribune* about the arrest spurred more rumors and fed into the tense frenzy in the city. People in the city were already insolent because of a hanging that had occurred earlier in the year.

A mob of white men marched down to the jail to demand a lynching. They were confronted by seventy-five armed Black men who were guarding the jail to make sure no one got hanged because of peer pressure. The sheriff tried to oversee the growing mob and proclaimed neither side needed to be there. The law had everything under control, and nobody would be hanged without a fair trial.

The Oklahoma City Bombing. *Photograph courtesy of the FBI website.*

It looked like both sides were going to listen to the sheriff, and people started to disperse. However, tempers were still high, and an older white man demanded that a Black man named O.B. Mann hand over his gun. Mann refused to give the pistol up because he was not going to listen to a white man who was trying to force him into something. The older white man tried to disarm him, and he was hit with a bullet in the process.

With tensions already high, the kerfuffle turned into a showdown. Shots blasted through the air on both sides. When the dust cleared and everyone was accounted for, twelve men ended up dead. This caused more mayhem, and the mob moved into other parts of the city to get revenge for those who had perished.

Rioters went into the mostly Black-populated Greenfield area. White men shot at innocent bystanders, destroyed property, looted stores and even ransacked private homes.

At around noon on June 1, the National Guard moved into Tulsa and declared martial law. Finally, the riot diffused, and people went back into their own neighborhoods.

It is estimated around ten thousand people were left homeless and more than $1.5 million (in 1921 currency) of property damage had occurred in the area. The fire and rubble spanned thirty-five city blocks, and over eight hundred people were hospitalized.

In the end, the Black shoeshiner named Rowland was cleared of all charges. According to the 1921 Race Riot Commission, there was no evidence against him, and the charges were highly suspect from the very beginning. They had no circumstantial evidence to support the claim of rape. He had not even been with the woman in the elevator long enough to have assaulted her.

The Oklahoma City Bombings

On April 19, 1995, at exactly 9:02 a.m., a bomb exploded in front of the Alfred P. Murrah Federal Building in Oklahoma City, Oklahoma. One-third of the building had been blasted to debris, and many of the floors disintegrated in the blink of an eye. Cars nearby were destroyed, and over three hundred buildings in the surrounding areas had been damaged in the explosion. Several hundred people walked away injured, and 168 people lost their lives, including nineteen children.

At first, the news and the general population assumed the bombing had been committed by Middle Eastern terrorists. However, within twenty-four hours, the FBI had found enough evidence to realize the bombing had come from a United States citizen. It was a terrible case of homegrown terrorism.

The investigation team discovered the explosive detonated in a rented Ryder van that was parked in front of the federal building. Among the rubble the FBI found the van's axle with the vehicle identification number on it. This would be the piece of evidence that broke the case wide open.

They traced the vehicle identification number to an auto body shop in Junction City, Kansas. Employees at the shop helped the FBI with a description of the person who had rented the van days earlier. They described him as a tall younger man with light brown hair and blue eyes. With the added information, officials were able to put together a sketch of the suspected bomber.

The FBI took the sketch to local businesses in the area to see if they could positively identify the man in the sketch or give them information about the whereabouts of the man. A hotel employee knew who the man was and even had his name: Timothy McVeigh.

McVeigh was an ex–army soldier who meticulously planned out and created a bomb for the terrorist attack. He created the bomb out of fertilizer, diesel fuel and other easily accessible chemicals, most of which you could buy at a hardware store. The terrorist left the explosive in the van, locked the door, got in his getaway car and detonated the bomb. He thought he had gotten away with it, too.

In a weird turn of events, the FBI did not have to hunt for McVeigh. The bomber was apprehended by a state trooper about eighty miles outside of Oklahoma City for not having a license plate on his car. McVeigh was arrested for carrying a concealed weapon and already booked in the local jail.

During a formal investigation with over 1,400 investigators and over three tons of evidence, the FBI found that McVeigh did not act alone. He had two other coconspirators: Terry Nichols and Michael Fortier. Nichols received a life sentence and Fortier got twelve years, but on January 20, 2006, Fortier left prison after serving just under eleven years. The FBI immediately put him and his family into a witness protection program, where he will live the rest of his life.

Fortier was by no means innocent, but he and his wife had pertinent information on McVeigh and cooperated with authorities. He had known about the bombings nine months before they happened. McVeigh had mapped out a diagram with soup cans in Fortier's kitchen to show how he was going to bomb the government building for maximum damage. The accomplice even staked out the area with McVeigh, helping him figure out where to park the van and other details.

During the investigation after the bombing, Fortier bragged on tapped phone conversations about how he was going to make $1 million off the movie rights for his story. He criticized the FBI and how they were investigating the case.

His wife, Lori Fortier, also helped McVeigh in his plot by helping him make a fake driver's license to rent the Ryder truck he used in the bombing. She also watching him build the bomb model. As part of her husband's plea bargain, she did not have to serve any time.

Michael Fortier ended up going to jail for lying to FBI agents, failing to alert officials on a homegrown terrorist plot and selling a stolen gun to finance an attack.

In 1994, Terry Nichols was convicted of conspiracy to use a weapon of mass destruction and eight counts of involuntary manslaughter for killing government personnel. He received life in prison because the jury was deadlocked on the death penalty. In 2004, he was convicted of 161 counts

Right: Timothy McVeigh being taken into custody. *Photograph courtesy of the FBI website.*

Below: The Survivor Tree. *From Wikimedia Commons.*

of first-degree murder, including fetal homicide; first-degree arson; and conspiracy. He received 161 consecutive life sentences with no possibility of parole. He was taking to a maximum-security prison in Florence, Colorado, on a cell block called "Bombers Row," which also houses Ramzi Yousef and Eric Rudolph.

McVeigh joined the army right after high school. There, he met Nichols, and the two became fast friends. In 1991, the soldier fought in the Gulf War and won medals for a combat mission. Despite the awards, McVeigh was discharged after just one year of service because of downsizing.

On June 2, 1997, he was convicted of fifteen counts of murder and conspiracy. Then in August of the same year, the bomber was sentenced to death by lethal injection. Appeals for his death sentence started immediately. However, in August 2000, McVeigh went in front of judge and asked that all appeals stop immediately and said his death date should be scheduled. In June 2001, McVeigh died by lethal injection at the U.S. Penitentiary at Terre Haute, Indiana. It was the first execution carried out from a federal death penalty sentence since 1963.

The Survivor Tree

The Survivor Tree is an elm tree in downtown Oklahoma City that sits directly across the street from the Alfred P. Murrah building. It survived the bomb blast from the Oklahoma City bombing. According to Foresters, the elm tree was planted sometime around 1920.

Prior to the terrorist attack, the tree was the only shaded area near the government building. People would come early just to have a chance to park underneath it.

Pieces of shrapnel from the bomb were hanging from the branches of the elm, and it was nearly chopped down. However, the FBI decided to save the tree because people in the area had so much love for it.

When construction of the Oklahoma City bombing memorial building started, it was specified that the plans must include the tree because it was an important part of the story and a symbol of hope. It persevered, much like the city and its people.

Saplings and seeds of the Survivor Tree have been made available to keep the legacy of the tree alive. For pictures of the tree throughout the years and information on how to visit the memorial, visit this website: https://memorialmuseum.com/experience/the-survivor-tree/.

PART I
LEGENDS AND LORE

Oklahoma has a rich history of Native American lore from a myriad of tribes that settled in the area because of the Indian Removal Act of the late 1800s and the subsequent Trail of Tears. Along with their heritage came their gods, goddesses and supernatural beings. Some of these paranormal creatures are helpful and cheeky like the "little" people," and others are downright terrifying and will eat your heart while it's still pumping blood like the Stikini. Others will lure into you the woods only to kill you—but only if you are a certain type of man. If you are of good moral character, then you don't need to worry.

There are supernatural forces in Oklahoma that encapsulated the land. They will suck you into portals or have you chasing lights during a dark night in the middle of the forest. These forces are intriguing and enigmatic because for hundreds of years, no one has ever discovered their true nature.

The following are a handful of Oklahoma's most interesting legends and lore.

1

THE YUNWI TSUNSDI

In Cherokee lore, the *Yunwi Tsunsdi* or "little people" are small humanoid nature spirits that live in the mountain rock eaves or small caves in the woods of Oklahoma. Their houses are located underground with tunnels between each resident. They burrow out little communities.

The Yunwi Tsunsdi have magical abilities. They are mostly invisible and only show themselves at their own whim or if they fancy you. They reach about knee height and have handsome features and hair that falls to the ground. Some are black, others are white and some are said to be golden like the Cherokee.

The little people are whimsical, mischievous little creatures that love music. Some have said they hear drumming and singing in the forest, but they can't pinpoint the exact source of the sound. When they go toward the music, it gets farther way, like it is traveling through the woods. These are the sounds of the little pretty people playing pranks on unsuspecting humans. They think it is funny to watch someone lurking through the forest looking for music, which they will never find. It is even funnier if the person gets lost and can't find their way out.

According to legend, the Yunwi Tsunsdi are broken up into three separate clans.

THE ROCK CLAN

These are the most vengeful and vindictive of the little people. They are quick to get offended and will get even just as quickly. The Rock Clan are

The Little People. *Drawing by Rebecca Lindsey.*

known to steal human children. They also throw rocks at people who take things out of the woods without their permission.

THE LAUREL CLAN

These are the most benevolent and fun little people. They are tricksters and love to play games with the unsuspecting. The Laurels are childlike and love to laugh. They also love making children laugh.

THE DOGWOOD CLAN

These are the most willing little people; they often show themselves and deal with humans. The Dogwoods will help humans out of the forest and show them pathways if needed. They have a profoundly serious nature and prefer to be left alone.

According to lore, the Yunwi Tsunsdi migrated to Oklahoma with the Native Americans during the Trail of Tears. They made their home here to help the Cherokee make a new home and to watch over them.

If you are in the Oklahoma forest and hear some music off in the distance, it is probably best if you don't go looking for its source. It is probably the little people playing a good prank. Make sure you watch your children if you are at the edge of the forest and leave if rocks are tossed at you for no reason. It means the rock clan is nearby, and they want your babies. If you want to appease the Yunwi Tsunsdi, bring them honey or milk and leave them near a tree.

2

THE STIKINI (OWL MAN)

Owls are creepy enough. They can nearly turn their heads completely around, and some of them sleep face down like they are dead. In certain lore, the cry of an owl is a portent of death. The legend of the *Stikini* takes owl lore up a notch into the realm of terror.

According to the Seminole, the Stikini is a vampiric creature that takes the form of a normal human being by day and an owl looking for prey at night.

The Seminole are a Native American tribe that originated in Florida but were relocated to Oklahoma during the Trail of Tears. Now, there are tribes in both regions. The Seminole are most known for their Green Corn Dance and tobacco rituals. Their Nation Tribal Complex exists in Wewoka, Oklahoma, which is about forty-five miles outside of Oklahoma City.

The Stikini transform in the most gruesome way. They vomit up their entrails and then hang them high up in a tree so that no other animals can eat them. Then they turn into an owl and go in search of an easy victim.

The Stikini look for humans who are asleep or in a vulnerable state. When they find their prey, the vampire owl will rip their heart out through their mouth and then leave the bloody body for someone else to find. After the Stikini is done feeding, it will go back to its entrails, swallow them whole and return to its human state.

In certain lore, the Stikini is a human witch who willingly does damning deeds to spread evil to become more powerful. At night, they regurgitate their souls, their blood and their organs before transforming into the vampiric

Stikini (Owl Man). *Drawing by Rebecca Lindsey.*

owl. They have unnatural super strength and can easily rip a person in two without even trying. The Stikini were so terrible that it was frowned upon to say the word for fear of conjuring one up—or worse, bringing the curse of becoming one upon oneself. Due to this, the Stikini were only spoken about through a medicine man who could protect themselves from such supernatural evil.

If you were to run into a Stikini in its human form, it would be hard to tell them apart from anyone else, except their moral compass may be a little off. They do not care about average social norms or traditions. So, the shapeshifter will be an outsider and live outside of the town or keep to themselves.

To kill a Stikini, you must find their entrails hanging in the tree and destroy them. Once destroyed, the vampiric owl will not be able to shapeshift back into its human form. It will eventually die from sunlight exposure.

3

THE LEGEND OF
JOHN WILKES BOOTH

This is not Native American lore, but it's a great tale, one that will keep your head spinning and your conspiracy theories turning. This story spans decades and involves an embalmed corpse that has seen more than most living people.

In 1903, in a small town called Enid, a man named David E. George died by suicide in one of the rooms at the Grand Avenue Hotel. A doctor diagnosed the cause of death as self-administered arsenic poisoning. Locals said they had seen the man buying strychnine earlier that morning at the drugstore.

George's body was moved to the Penniman's Furniture Store, which also happened to be the city funeral home. It was embalmed and propped up in a chair in the window of the furniture store so the public could view it. Someone took a picture.

The members of the coroner's jury heard all kinds of weird stories about George during their inquiry. He had access to money but ended up dying penniless. He touted himself as a house painter but did not know how to paint. He was a loner who quoted Shakespeare and was known for saying, "I killed the best man that ever lived."

So, who was this guy? Why were so many people interested in him even after his death? This is where the story gets interesting.

Two days after George's death, Reverend E.C. Harper came into town to identify the body. Based on the description, he assumed the body was to be of the solitary man who frequented the town bar and loved

Side-by-side photographs of the mummified corpse of David E. George (*left*) and John Wilkes Booth (*right*). *From Wikimedia Commons, collage by Heather Woodward.*

alcohol. However, when he saw the body in person, he stated to undertaker W.H. Ryan, "This is the body of John Wilkes Booth, the man who killed Abraham Lincoln."

John Wilkes Booth was an accomplished and popular actor of the time. His father was a well-known British Shakespearean actor who came to the United States with his lover in 1821. They purchased a 150-acre plot in Bel Air, Maryland, and built a four-bedroom log house. Booth was born on May 10, 1828. He was the ninth of ten children. He was a popular boy and good in sports. He excelled in equestrian sports and fencing. Booth was not the best student in school, but he took advantage of the educational opportunities he had and did the best he could with them.

When he was around fourteen years old, Booth met a Romani fortuneteller who read his palm. The fortuneteller told him that he would have short but grand life. He was doomed to die young. His sister stated he wrote down the prediction and took it to heart.

At seventeen, Booth started his acting career. At first, he failed, flubbing lines in his debut role in *Richard III*. However, over the years, he kept at it and became a well-seasoned, well-liked actor. He was known for his good looks and charm. Legend states that women swooned in his presence, and he became a box office draw.

Booth hated the abolishment of slavery and resented President Lincoln for his part in it. He became part of a group of Confederate sympathizers and conspirators who wanted to take the president out. Their original plan was to kidnap President Lincoln in exchange for Confederate prisoners. That fell through, and instead, Booth shot the president at the Ford Theater on April 14, 1865. Lincoln died the next day at 7:22 a.m. after being in a coma for eight hours.

After Booth shot Lincoln, he jumped off the stage, and legend states he broke his right leg. He escaped by jumping on a horse and riding to southern Maryland. Twelve days later, the assassin was found holed up in a North Carolina barn. According to the official story, the barn was set on fire. Seargent Boston Corbett of the Sixteenth New York Cavalry shot and killed Booth, even though his orders were to bring him in alive so he could face a proper trial.

However, errors were made concerning the identification of Booth's body. One of the main errors involved Corbett, the man who allegedly shot Booth, as he was one of the only persons to officially identify the corpse. This did not go over well with the public, since they felt Corbett had a vested interest in saying it was Booth, whether it was or not. People thought he was not above lying to make himself look good.

In 1953, Helen Jo Banks authored a thesis at Oklahoma State University that proposed the government's hurried identification process left the public questioning whether Booth was alive from the very start. Rumors started to circulate just days after it was announced that Corbett shot Booth while he was fleeing from the burning barn.

Some stories posited that the assassin fled the barn alive and escaped while the man who died was a farmhand named Ruddy who had been sent to get some of Booth's personal belongings. Those who were at the scene and saw the dead body said it looked nothing like Booth, which got the rumors circulating quickly.

SURRAT.   BOOTH.   HAROLD.

War Department, Washington, April 20, 1865,

 ## $100,000 REWARD!

THE MURDERER

Of our late beloved President, Abraham Lincoln,

IS STILL AT LARGE.

$50,000 REWARD

Will be paid by this Department for his apprehension, in addition to any reward offered by Municipal Authorities or State Executives.

$25,000 REWARD

Will be paid for the apprehension of JOHN H. SURRATT, one of Booth's Accomplices.

$25,000 REWARD

Will be paid for the apprehension of David C. Harold, another of Booth's accomplices.

LIBERAL REWARDS will be paid for any information that shall conduce to the arrest of either of the above-named criminals, or their accomplices.

All persons harboring or secreting the said persons, or either of them, or aiding or assisting their concealment or escape, will be treated as accomplices in the murder of the President and the attempted assassination of the Secretary of State, and shall be subject to trial before a Military Commission and the punishment of DEATH.

Let the stain of innocent blood be removed from the land by the arrest and punishment of the murderers.

All good citizens are exhorted to aid public justice on this occasion. Every man should consider his own conscience charged with this solemn duty, and rest neither night nor day until it be accomplished.

EDWIN M. STANTON, Secretary of War.

DESCRIPTIONS.—BOOTH is Five Feet 7 or 8 inches high, slender build, high forehead, black hair, black eyes, and wears a heavy black moustache.

JOHN H. SURRAT is about 5 feet, 9 inches. Hair rather thin and dark; eyes rather light; no beard. Would weigh 145 or 150 pounds. Complexion rather pale and clear, with color in his cheeks. Wore light clothes of fine quality. Shoulders square; check bones rather prominent; chin narrow; ears projecting at the top; forehead rather low and square, but broad. Parts his hair on the right side; neck rather long. His lips are firmly set. A slim man.

DAVID C. HAROLD is five feet six inches high, hair dark, eyes dark, eyebrows rather heavy, full face, nose short, hand short and fleshy, feet small, instep high, round bodied, naturally quick and active, slightly closes his eyes when looking at a person.

NOTICE.—In addition to the above, State and other authorities have offered rewards amounting to almost one hundred thousand dollars, making an aggregate of about TWO HUNDRED THOUSAND DOLLARS.

John Wilkes Booth reward poster from 1865. *From Getty Images.*

It is rumored that Booth traveled through the United States with a slew of different aliases, guided by his fellow Confederate sympathizers. It is said he ended up in Enid, Oklahoma, and the rest is history—or is it? Because the story gets stranger.

While George's body remained propped up in the window of the furniture store, Finis L. Bates, a lawyer from Tennessee, spotted the body and identified it as his friend John St. Helen. He had known St. Helen (George) as a client for over five years in Granbury, Texas. St. Helen had gotten terribly ill, to the point that he thought he was going to die. He had asked to see Bates alone because he had a confession to make.

He quietly stated, "I am dying. My name is John Wilkes Booth, and I am the assassin of President Lincoln."

St. Helen explained that Vice President Andrew Johnson had created the assassination plot and that he was given a password to escape the fugitive hunt. He escaped the barn fire and traveled across the West with different aliases. Bates explained that St. Helen ended up not dying and got better. Soon after he recovered, he left town quickly.

This was not the only deathbed confession from the man with a bunch of names. According to an article in a Memphis newspaper, nine months before George's death, a minister's wife had been at the bed of a man who had tried to die by suicide. He whispered to her, "I am not David Elihu George. I am J. Wilkes Booth."

George would try to kill himself again in 1903 and succeeded.

Due to the popularity of these deathbed confessionals, the body of George remained in the window of the furniture store for the rest of the year. In 1904, the body was displayed at the St. Louis World's Fair.

In 1907, Bates, the lawyer, penned the book *The Life and Suicide of John Wilkes Booth: Written for the Correction of History*, which told the story of St. Helen's accounts of what happened during Booth's fugitive hunt, and the history of George included his suicide. Bates gained custody of George's embalmed corpse and rented it out to freak shows throughout the United States.

In 1920, the cadaver was stolen off a train that had crashed on its way to California and was held for ransom. Bates retrieved the mummified corpse and continued to hock it out to sideshows. However, the body started to gain its own dark mythos.

According to a 1938 copy of the *Saturday Evening Post*, the body "scattered ill luck around almost as freely as Tutankhamen is supposed to have done." The article went on to say that every entertainer who had ever exhibited

Side-by-side photographs of John St. Helen (*left*) and John Wilkes Booth (*right*). *Collage by Heather Woodward.*

the body went into financial ruin. A set of Union veterans tried to steal the corpse and threatened to lynch it.

In 1923, Bates died, and his widow sold the corpse to William Evan, the Carnival Kid of the Southwest, who took the body to his potato farm. He created a sign that said, "SEE THE MAN WHO MURDERED LINCOLN," and exhibited it there. Evans tried to tour with George's embalmed body, but interest had fizzled out by then.

In the 1930s, John Harkin bought the body for $5,000 and traveled around the United States with it. He offered up $1,000 to anyone who could prove the body was not that of John Wilkes Booth. In 1931, the corpse was X-rayed by a group of Chicago doctors. They claimed that the neck scar, broken thumb and broken leg were consistent with a description of Booth's body.

From 1937 to sometime in the 1950s, the mummified body belonged to Jay Gould's Million-Dollar Circus and traveled through the United States. According to PBS, the body was last seen sometime in the late 1970s and is now in someone's private collection.

Was David E. George really John Wilkes Booth? We may never know.

According to the *Oklahoma Gold* podcast, the Booth family has tried to work with the government and the courts to get DNA testing, but to no avail. When Booth's body went through an autopsy, three vertebrae were removed from his body and were put on display for years.

A postcard of David E. George in the window of the furniture store in Enid, Oklahoma. *Originally posted in the* Enid News and Eagle.

The Booth family repeatedly asked the government to test the vertebrae against a relative to make sure the right man had died. The government ignored the requests. So, the family took the matter to court.

Finally, after years of querying, a judge declared they could do the testing. The Booth family contacted the government and asked for the vertebrae so they could be tested. The government said the three vertebrae had disappeared and that they were not able to hand them over because they no longer had them in their possession.

Cue the *X-Files* music, because this sounds an awful lot like a conspiracy.

4

THE CENTER OF THE UNIVERSE

1 SOUTH BOSTON AVENUE
TULSA, OKLAHOMA 74103

Despite its spectacular name, the Center of the Universe is an average-looking round piece of concrete about thirty inches in diameter surrounded by several circles of bricks. It's what it does that makes it interesting.

If you stand in the middle of the concrete circle and use your voice in any way, the sound is amplified and reverberates like a personal echo chamber. However, anyone outside of the circle will think you are speaking in a normal tone and will not hear the amplification.

The Center of the Universe sits on a walking bridge that connects the Greenwood District to downtown Tulsa. The bridge was once a vehicular bridge until the 1980s, when it burned down in a fire. Considered an anomaly, the Center of the Universe was created through the placement of a circle along the expansion joint of the new bridge. According to the Tulsa Foundation of Architecture, the echo feature could be created by the concrete planters that surround the brick circle.

Some visitors believe the Center of the Universe is the apex of a vortex where cosmic energies converge. Others think it is a gathering place for trickster ghosts that like to play with sound. For instance, people believe that if you drop a small object, like a pin, in the middle of the echo chamber, it will sound like a giant crash instead of tiny tinny *tink* sound. To this day, nobody really knows the real reason the Center of the Universe exists. It defies all the laws of physics.

Center of the Universe in Tulsa, Oklahoma. *Picture taken by Heather Woodward.*

Author's Experience at Center of the Universe

I took my mother to the experience the Center of the Universe. She had never heard of it and thought it was something the locals made up to lure in gullible tourists. The area is easy to find. You can type in "center of the universe" in Google Maps or Waze and the directions pop right up.

When you get to the area, you must park on the street and walk a few hundred yards. The area is marked by a seventy-two-and-a-half-foot-tall sculpture called *Artificial Cloud*, which was created by Native American artist Robert Haozous. According to the description from the Tulsa Convention and Visitor's Bureau, it is a commentary on man's destructive infatuation with technology. It was created to welcome rust and wear by weather and time. It is an interesting sculpture, albeit a little creepy. There are these things that look like little people running down one side and a fleet of airplanes sort of falling haphazardly on the other. It looks like, at any moment, the men and the airplanes will converge in a fiery ball of doom.

The Center of the Universe itself is not spectacular or fancy. It's a blink-and-you'll-miss-it anomaly.

My mom walked up to it and said, "That's it?"

She was skeptical because it is basically just a round circle in the concrete surrounded by bricks. I walked into the circle and started to talk. I could hear my voice reverberating like I was in an amphitheater. My voice was loud.

I asked my mom if I sounded any different and she said no. So, we switched. She stood in the circle, and she said her voice was echoing, but I could not hear it.

It was the strangest thing.

I went back into the circle and recorded myself. In the circle. I could hear my voice reverberating, but it did not pick up on the audio. For some reason, the effect only works in person.

You can listen to the audio here: https://bit.ly/centeroftheuniverse.

If you are in the Tulsa area, be sure to check out the Center of the Universe. It is an interesting anomaly and something you should experience in real life.

5

SHAMAN PORTAL

BEAVER DUNES PARK
US 270
BEAVER, OKLAHOMA 73932

Considered the "Bermuda Triangle of Oklahoma," the Beaver Dunes Park is a three-hundred-acre recreational oasis for ATVs and off-road vehicles. However, it also hosts one of the creepiest supernatural legends in the state.

During the 1500s, Spanish explorer Francisco Vazquez de Coronado traveled through the sand dunes. Three of his men suddenly disappeared without a trace in front of him while he witnessed it. According to his journal, "it was the work of the Devil," as his men had vanished in a flash of green lightning.

The Native American guides working with Coronado warned him not to go through the dunes because the area was evil. They nicknamed the location the "Shaman's Portal" and had avoided it for centuries. Coronado was not a superstitious man and ignored the warnings of the locals. His men paid the cost of his careless decision-making.

Legend says other men have seen the green lighting and have mysteriously disappeared in the sand dunes, never to be seen again. Theories suggest the green lights are the first signs of an interdimensional portal opening. People are accidentally sucked into it and taken to another dimension, where they spend the rest of their days in utter confusion. Some say that the sand dunes are home to an ancient Native American burial ground and that is why the portal exists. The portal takes you into the netherworld.

If portals to other dimensions are not enough, there's an even stranger tale about the sand dunes. Locals say there is a UFO buried the area. Some

Coronado Sets Out the North, oil painting by Frederic Remington, circa 1890s. *From Wikimedia Commons.*

have witnessed strange, unexplained excavations in the middle of the night by people clad in military-looking regalia. In the 1990s, Oklahoma State University archaeologist Dr. Mark Thatcher spent three years studying and excavating the area. He was shut down by government officials who eerily resembled the notorious MIB or Men in Black.

Also during the nineties, a number of soil samples were taken in the area. Allegedly, they showed strange anomalies, including ionized soil and electromagnetic interference. Areas with frequent UFO sightings tend to have these kinds of radiation traces in their soil. Other theories have suggested the sand dunes are on top of a set of major ley lines, and the energy from them feeds the portal. It also attracts alien visitation.

If you end up staying at Beaver Park, watch out for green lights and strange men in black suits, unless you want to suddenly disappear. But it is probably for the best that you stay out of the area all together.

6

THE SPOOK LIGHT

There is no specific address, but here are some directions: on Highway 144, take Exit 4, Highway 86 South. Drive six miles to Route BB. Turn right on BB Highway until it ends, then turn right. Drive one mile, then turn left on E50 Road (Spook Light Road). About two miles down E50, you will find the best place to see the light.

The Spook Light is a basketball-sized orb located in a small area called "Devil's Promenade" between the borders of Missouri and Oklahoma. It can be witnessed from Quapaw, Oklahoma, but because it tends to be eastbound, people have also associated it with Hornet, Missouri.

The Spook Light usually shows up as a singular fiery ball that bobs and weaves down the road at high speeds, then moves through the tops of the trees and disappears. People have seen the ball of light show up as mostly green or blue but also with a red or orange hue. The best time to experience the moving orb is between the hours of 10:00 p.m. and midnight. The Spook Light will not show up around loud noises or large group. You must be quiet and go alone.

The first encounter with the Spook Light dates to the time of the Trail of Tears in the 1830s. However, the first documented sighting occurred in 1881, and a recounting appeared in a publication called *Ozark Spook Light*.

Lore says the light comes from a Native American tale in which two lovers are looking for each other, hoping to reunite. It is very Romeo and Juliet. A Quapaw maiden fell in love with a young man. Her father would not allow

The Spook Light. *Drawing by Rebecca Lindsey.*

her to marry him because his dowry wasn't large enough. The maiden went against her father, and the couple eloped. The father sent warriors after the couple to bring them back to the tribe and break them up. They were almost apprehended, but instead, they jumped off a cliff together because they would rather die than live apart.

Another legend says an Osage Native leader had his head decapitated. The bobbing and weaving light is said to be his lantern held high up where his head would be. He's searching the area, looking for his lost head.

Explanations for the Spook Light range from luminous gases, car lights and electrical atmospheric charges to fault lines. In 1946, the U.S. Army Corps of Engineers studied the orb of light and could not find an explanation for it. So far, no theory has been definitive.

According to locals, the Spook Light is a consistent phenomenon. There is an extremely high chance you will be able to witness it if you follow the rules. Park on the side of the road, remain quiet and do not bring a lot of people. If you are respectful, it will show itself to you. Then you can spend the rest of the evening with a conspiracy board, trying to figure out what the Spook Light is and how it works.

PART II

GHOSTS AND GHOULS

Where there is history, there are ghosts, and Oklahoma has its share. Surprising to many who visit, the state has an abundance of brick-faced buildings that resemble much of the old neighborhoods on the East Coast. This is because the Freemasons have hung their hats in the Sooner State.

The first Freemason lodge in Oklahoma was built in Tahlequah, the last stop on the Trail of Tears. It is now the headquarters of the Cherokee Nation. The governing grand lodge for the Freemasons resides in Guthrie, which also happens to be one of the most haunted towns in the United States. If you go to Guthrie, you will feel the energy shift as soon as you hit the town.

Is it a coincidence that the Freemasons built their grand lodge in a city known for its hauntings? Probably. However, it could also be that the area is a giant hub of ley lines and energy that functions as a battery for the other side.

There are many ghosts in Oklahoma, and many provide familiar tales that you will hear in every small town with a prolific history. There are the ladies in white, the giggling children and the man with cigar smoke. But then there are those tales that are born from real history and, for some, true crime cases. Even the crying bridges have ghosts stemming from real-life events.

The Hex House history, for instance, is so notorious and outlandish, a haunted attraction in Tulsa, Oklahoma, is named after it. An old "For Sale" sign sits next to the old brick stairs, inviting someone to take a chance on the hexed property. The plot of land on which it used to reside cannot be sold because no one wants to risk buying it.

The Stone Lion Inn is home to the ghost of a mischievous child playing on its third floor. But which child is it? Is it little Augusta or little Irene? The stories get twisted and retold over time, and now there is a history in the building that's all its own.

Read among these pages the twists and turns of Oklahoma history. Visit one of these locations if you dare. You will not be disappointed. You just might get the fright of your life.

7

CRYBABY BRIDGE

The following are the two Crybaby Bridges in Oklahoma with the easiest access and the most activity. You can drive right near them with your car and then reach them by foot. Make sure to bring an audio recorder to catch EVPs or use one on your phone.

CRYBABY BRIDGE 1: CATOOSA BOGGY CREEK BRIDGE

This bridge is located on South Keetonville Road.
   For specifics, visit: https//bridgehunter.com/ok/rogers/boggy-creek/.

CRYBABY BRIDGE 2

Kellyville directions: From Kellyville, drive west on Route 66 for a half mile, take a left on Slick Road. Drive 1.1 miles. At Polecat Creek, the bridge will be on the left-hand side.
   There are a handful of Crybaby Bridges in Oklahoma, and the stories attached to the bridges come from real-life wrongful death cases. A woman died by suicide after throwing herself and her baby over the bridge. In another case, a woman threw a baby over the railing into the creek below to a gruesome death. In yet another case, a woman crashed her car and plummeted to her death with her baby in the seat beside her.

There are urban legends, too. One is about a witch who takes children. Oh, and there is another legend in which the witch lived in the adjoining woods and started a fire. Each has their own spin, but the most common attribute of all these Crybaby Bridges is the sound of a baby hitting the water from down below, the screams of a wailing woman and the guttural cries of an infant.

The Crybaby Bridges are located in Catoosa, Alderson, Checotah, Hontubby, Bixby, Lawton, Vinita, Kellyville (considered the original) and Moore.

The Crybaby Bridge in Catoosa is called Boggy Creek Bridge. On June 13, 1924, during a vicious rainstorm, a woman and her baby were crossing the bridge in a horse-drawn buggy. A whip of thunder and lightning cracked in the sky. The excited horses bucked and flipped the carriage over. Both the mom and baby were tossed in a frenzy of movement and chaos.

Frantic, the woman searched wildly for her baby. She heard a crying baby down below in the swelling river. Scared for her baby's life, the woman ran to the edge of the bridge and leaned over. In her haste, she slipped, went over bridge and fell into the river. Both the woman and the baby disappeared, never to be seen again.

People in the area say that if you go to the bridge on any given Friday the Thirteenth, you can hear the cries of the baby, who is still looking for their mother.

Every year in June, during the days after the accident, red roses used to appear on two unmarked graves near the edge of the river. The roses stopped when someone wrote "Bessie" and "Clissie" on the graves. Perhaps they are the names of the two victims of the bridge accident.

If you end up going to one of the Crybaby Bridges, make sure you dress accordingly. Wear jeans, long-sleeve shirts and sturdy boots. Most of the bridges are located in overgrown wooded areas and are in disrepair because they are not used anymore. Be careful if you are going to try to walk on any of the bridges. It would be better to hang out underneath the bridge in the creek beds or at the edge of the water. That is where the anomalous sounds are usually witnessed.

8

DEAD WOMAN'S CROSSING

The name Dead Woman's Crossing conjures up images of a spooky location infused with local lore and legend. Except this place is named after a strange and tragic true crime case.

On July 7, 1905, a schoolteacher named Kate DeWitt James and her fourteen-month-old baby boarded a train in Custer City, Oklahoma, to visit her cousin who lived in Ripley, Oklahoma. She boarded the train the day after she filed divorce from her abusive husband because she was ready to start a new life. Her father, Henry DeWitt, took her to the train station and asked her to contact him when she got to her cousin's house. He wanted to make sure she made it safely and wanted to know how she liked settling into her new abode.

Two weeks went by, and DeWitt never got any kind of communication from his daughter. Anxious and fearful of the worst, he hired private investigator Sam Bartell to find his daughter and her baby. Bartell started his investigation in Clinton, Oklahoma, but no one had seen the schoolteacher or her baby in the area.

On July 28, 1905, the private investigator went to Weatherford, Oklahoma. He found out James had gotten off the train with a prostitute named Frannie Norton (also known as Ms. Ham) and stayed the night at the house of William Moore. Moore was the brother of Norton's husband.

In the early morning hours of the day the schoolteacher went missing, witnesses described seeing Norton driving James in a buggy toward Hydro, Oklahoma. They had taken a route that passed over Deer Creek. About

The highway bridge over Dead Woman's Crossing. *From Shutterstock.*

forty-five minutes later, Norton stopped at Moore's house and then went back to her home in Clinton, Oklahoma. One of the wheels of the buggy had something that looked like blood splattered on it.

Bartell had a hunch about what had happened to the schoolteacher, but he still had not figured out what had happened to the baby. After some sleuthing, he discovered that Norton had dropped the baby off with a boy on a farm. She asked the boy to take care of the baby until someone came for her. Fortunately, the infant was unharmed, but her clothes were covered in blood.

Bartell searched for Norton and had her taken into custody. She denied knowing what happened to James. After a day of questioning, the prostitute went home and died by suicide after consuming poison.

In August, a man who was fishing with his son found a fully clothed headless skeleton under a wood wagon crossing over Deer Creek. The head was lying three feet away and had a .38-caliber bullet hole behind the right ear. A gun was discovered a few yards away.

The running theory was that Norton had taken James to the creek to kill her under the guise that she was taking her to her cousin's house. She pulled the gun out and shot the schoolteacher in the head and then gave the baby to the first person she saw. Norton did not take any of James's belongings, so it wasn't a robbery. No one knows the real motive for killing James, and with Norton dead, nobody will ever know.

James's father and (almost ex) husband came into town to identify the remains of the skeleton. Unfortunately, the divorce had not been official because she had gone missing. Her husband took the baby and her estate.

Eighty years later, the wooden crossing was replaced by a concrete bridge. They named it Dead Woman's Crossing after James. Her memory lived on, even though she did not.

Some reports say James's spirit has been seen roaming the bridge and heard calling out for her baby. Others have reported that if you stand under the bridge, you can hear the rickety wheels of Norton's buggy crossing over on the way to James's place of death.

The moral of this story is this: do not get off trains in unknown locations or befriend strangers. You never know when your head will turn up at the bottom of a creek.

9

HEX HOUSE

10 EAST TWENTY-FIRST STREET
TULSA, OKLAHOMA 74114

The Hex House's haunting is not tied so much to the structure itself but to the woman who lived in it. Her name was Carol Ann Smith; she was a middle-aged woman who lived in the ivy-covered duplex in Tulsa, Oklahoma. In 1944, she became a household name when she was investigated and later arrested for "hexing" two women, Virginia Evans and Willetta Horner, into giving their paychecks to her and living a life of slavery for the better part of eight years.

Neighbors were most curious about the arrest because for years, they had heard screams and strange noises, including growls, coming from the house. They had also seen an unidentified person cleaning a gun on the porch and the burial of a small casket in the backyard. When Smith was apprehended, her neighbors circled the house and gawked as she came out in cuffs.

When the police went through the house, they saw that there were two distinct kinds of lifestyles being led inside. While Smith lived a luxurious lifestyle, which included designer clothing, an expensive silverware set, over two hundred pairs of shoes, twenty-six hats and an obnoxious amount of makeup and toiletries, the two enslaved women lived in the unheated basement, slept on orange crates, lived in tattered clothing and were denied any kind of amenities, including makeup.

The women explained to the police that they were told if they gave Smith all their money, they would receive a "big payoff" in heaven. Smith had created her own religion in which the two women were starved and beaten periodically for spiritual purification. Evans went as far as to let Smith fictitiously take care of her "father" to bring in $17,000 in faux nursing care.

Aside from taking the paychecks of her two basement mates, Smith had life insurance policies taken out on her late father, her dead husband and her house cleaner, who had died under weird circumstances. Her husband was said to have died by suicide after shooting himself in the head, and the house cleaner was said to have depression and ran into oncoming traffic. The *Tulsa Tribune* called Smith the "she-Svengali of Oklahoma" because of her antics.

So, who was this woman who could manipulate and coax anyone to do anything? She was born Opal Mary Carey in Indianapolis, Indiana. Her mother had died when she was nine years old, and she was primarily raised by her father. Eventually, they moved to Muskogee, Oklahoma, where she met a well-known oil supply salesperson, Fay H. Smith. They were married very quickly, and Carol Ann had her first child in 1914. The baby did not live past a few days. She got pregnant again in 1919, and again, the baby did not live past the first week.

A side profile of the Hex House. *Drawing by Rebecca Lindsey.*

In 1920, the couple decided to start over and moved to Tulsa, Oklahoma. They happily stayed there until 1934, when Smith was laid off from his job as the country was in the throes of the Great Depression. Very shortly after his layoff, Smith was discovered dead by a gunshot wound to the head. He had allegedly used a twig to pull the trigger. The death was considered a suicide, and Carol Ann received a huge settlement from a life insurance policy she had taken out on him.

Friends and family couldn't believe Smith had died by suicide. People who knew him well said that he was an incredibly positive person and that he would never even consider ending his own life. It later came out that Carol Ann had a lengthy conversation with him about dying by suicide days before he pulled the trigger.

After Smith's death, Carol Ann's property owner raised the rent in an attempt to get her to move out. He had a bad feeling about her and did not want her on the premises now that her husband wasn't there as a buffer. His ruse worked, and she moved into the ivy-covered duplex at 10 East Twenty-First Street.

Claiming her house was too big to live in alone, Carol Ann asked her dad to live with her. He came to visit her from St. Louis, Missouri, regularly, and she suggested she could care for him more easily if they lived in the same house. Before he could officially move to Tulsa, Carol Ann's father died. Fortuitously, the spinster had taken out a life insurance policy on him during their negotiations, and she was paid handsomely for his demise.

Then in February 1935, a woman named Beulah Walker ran out of the Twenty-First Street duplex screaming and leaped into oncoming traffic. Due to the wounds she received after being hit by a car, she died in the hospital a few days later. Carol Ann said that the woman was a forty-five-year-old widowed nurse who lived with her. Investigators tried to find Walker's next of kin, but to no avail, so Carol Ann made all the funeral arrangements.

It was later discovered that Walker was the house cleaner and Carol Ann was the beneficiary of a life insurance policy that had been taken out on her. However, this policy was canceled when the Carol Ann tried to take out an extra claim, stating Walker was a wealthy aunt. The insurance company got suspicious and did a thorough investigation. When they found out that the dead woman was an underpaid employee of the spinster, they denied all of her claims.

Two years later, in 1937, Carol Ann met Evans in a Christian bookstore. They struck up a friendship, and Evans asked to move in with the widow. A year later, Carol Ann met Horner in a grocery store. Horner complained about her toxic family, and she asked Carol Ann if she would adopt her and let her live in the duplex. The rest, as they say, is history.

Carol Ann would have never been found out, except she got careless. Her official investigation was prompted by a neighbor who noticed that Smith had eight World War II ration booklets when there were only three people living in the house. She had booklets for herself, Horner, Evans, a few made-up people and one for a daughter named Bonnie. Her "daughter" ended up being her dog, Bon Bon, whose corpse was the one that was recovered in the backyard. The body was placed in a cardboard box about five feet underground.

In the house, Smith had books on magnetism, self-mastery and mind control. She also had writings on how to control people through witchcraft and magic. At the trial, when the women were asked why they stayed with Smith, Evans said she thought she was to give up her family so that

The concrete foundation where the Hex House used to sit, complete with the ever-present "For Sale" sign. *Public domain.*

the middle-aged woman could adopt her. Both women said that Smith punctuated everything with scripture, so they thought she was bringing them into a better life.

In the end, Smith received only one year of jail time. After her time in jail, Carol Ann left the state and disappeared from the limelight. The duplex was demolished in 1975, and the basement was filled in with dirt and paved over with cement. The original stairs remain intact.

Although the house isn't there anymore, people have described experiencing all kinds of strange activity in what is now a parking lot. Cars turn on and off by themselves. Engines sputter, and starters refuse to turn over. Windshield wipers and radios turn on without anyone in the car. And sometimes, cars end up disappearing and are found blocks away.

If you go to the Hex House, maybe you should walk.

AUTHOR'S EXPERIENCE AT THE HEX HOUSE

I went to the Hex House with my friend Stephanie as part of the Tulsa Spirit Tours' Serial Killers, Murder and Mayhem Bus Tour. Stephanie is an empath, psychic and channeler. She is very good at it. It was during the Halloween season, and we wanted to do something different and fun.

The bus tour started off strangely. We stopped at a stoplight in the middle of downtown Tulsa. I start to feel panicky, dizzy and sick to my stomach. At the same time, I felt dissociated from it and was not sure what was going on. The driver drove another block, and someone from the back of the bus started yelling about how they needed to get off right away.

Apparently, a man's daughter had a migraine, and riding in the bus gave her motion sickness. The bus swerved over to a curb, and the whole family jumped off the bus as fast as they could. As soon as the daughter hit cement, she began to vomit.

Our tour guide offered to stay until the daughter felt better, but the family decided to walk back to their car and call it a night. As soon as the girl got off the bus, my wave of panic and nausea instantly subsided.

I guess in my curious state, I went into empath mode and started channeling the weird energy of the girl in the back of the bus.

The Hex House no longer stands at the Twenty-First Street address. It is basically a concrete slab that is now used as a parking lot. The original stairs are still visible. They are steep. They lead directly to the sidewalk and then right into a main street. I can see how the house cleaner, Beulah Walker,

Looking at the stairs of the Hex House from the concrete foundation. *Photograph by Heather Woodward.*

had run out of the house and gotten hit. If she was in a hysterical state, she would have run out the door about twenty feet straight into traffic.

Our driver parked the bus over the slab where the basement used to be and did not turn off the ignition. Our guide said they stop at the same location every time they do the tour. One time, they turned off the ignition and the bus would not start. The lights stopped working as well. So they do not take chances anymore.

We were allowed to walk around, do a bit of paranormal sleuthing and take pictures. We got out of the bus thinking we would feel something sinister, tense or horrible. I have been in tons of haunted buildings and on plots of haunted land. There is an edgy kind of feeling that comes on right away. But nothing happened there. It was a really relaxing parking lot.

Stephanie and I decided to do a quick EVP session and ask a question to see if there were any spirits or residual energy on the lot.

On the recording I ask, "Is anyone here? Is there anything you want to say? Is this place truly haunted?"

After a couple of seconds Stephanie replies, "I keep hearing 'mind control, mind control, mind control.'"

We started asking about what kind of mind control Carol Ann used, what kind of rituals she did and if the rumors that she built bonfires and danced naked in the moonlight during full moons were true.

On the recording, while we are discussing mind control, there are sounds of someone running behind us—the distinct sound of heavy shoes or low heels running on pavement.

On the recording, you can hear the traffic. Cars were driving past the whole time. The shoes hitting pavement created sounds that were completely different to anything else on the audio. While writing this, I went back and listened to the shoe sounds about ten times to make sure that it was not the other people on the bus or more odd car sounds.

We asked some more questions.

Stephanie wanted to know the name of the woman. I answered Carol Ann.

Then I asked who was in the coffin that was buried in the backyard, even though I knew it is the dog, Bon Bon. I wanted to see if I could illicit a response.

On the recording, I mention that I begin to hear music, like there was always music playing in the house.

There is a bit of silence.

Then Stephanie says, "She liked it. She liked what she was doing. It was not just…a money thing. I think she liked having control…doing whatever the hell she wanted."

We have a conversation about the time. I see the numbers 444, which is a sign for Stephanie and me that something is afoot. It is like a metaphysical validation that we are on the right track.

I say to Stephanie, "I don't feel remorse at all. Not even the ladies in the basement."

Stephanie agrees. She says, "No."

I finish my thought, "I don't think they even care."

Stephanie suggests that the ladies knew what they were getting into. They were into doing the rituals. They liked the spiritual aspect of it.

Being in the energy of the Hex House, both of us thought the plot was haunted because of the rituals done there, not because of the atrocities. We thought it was residual energy.

We decided to take a picture of the stairs before we had to get back on the bus. On the recording, I can hear myself and Stephanie walking. It has the same crunching quality as the running sounds from earlier.

I can tell you without a doubt that no one was running around. We would have said something during the recording. And I know we ventured off by ourselves because we did not want to hear other people's conversations.

It is a weird little anomaly.

Is the Hex House plot haunted? Probably. But it is a subtle kind of haunting. It is not the "in your face," tense kind of haunting. If you go to the plot, make sure you have some time to sit and feel the energy. Be sure to bring a recorder and ask a lot of questions. Maybe read a book on mind control or witchcraft and see what happens. Just make sure to have your AAA card ready because your car may not start.

10

STONE LION INN

1016 SOUTH WARNER AVENUE
GUTHRIE, OKLAHOMA 73044

The Stone Lion Inn started out as a personal residence, built in 1907 by F.E. Houghton, who founded the Cotton Oil Company and owned the first car dealership in Oklahoma. He built the property on the plot next door to his other house, which he and his family had outgrown. At the time of their move-in, the Houghtons had six children. The house was eight thousand square feet and had four floors (including the basement). It cost $11,900, which was a lot of money back then. The average house in the area cost about $800 to build in the early 1900s. The Houghtons' was the largest and most expensive house in Guthrie, Oklahoma, at the time.

The story goes that tragedy struck shortly after the family moved into the house. Their eight-year-old daughter, Augusta, contracted whooping cough. Bedridden, the little girl was given copious amounts of coughing suppressant by one of the house cleaners. In those days, cough medications had opium and codeine in them, and unfortunately, she accidentally overdosed and died.

However, historical research shows that the story of Augusta may not be true—she never died in the house. Augusta may have been confused with a newborn who died around the same time she got sick. Or perhaps there was another sibling named Irene around the age of seven or eight who died of whooping cough in the house.

According to a 1900 census report, a child named Irene lived in the house, but she does not appear in another report from 1910. It is a sign that she is probably the child who died from an overdose in the house.

As far as death certificates go, the only one that confirms a death in the house is that of Mr. Houghton.

The Houghtons remained in the family home until the early 1920s, when it was leased out as a funeral home for eight years. It was called Smith Funeral Home, and the family of the same name lived on the third floor. They did the embalming in the kitchen and had the mortuary in the basement.

After being a funeral home, the home was once again occupied by the Houghtons. In 1943, Mr. Houghton died from a heart attack. It is said that he died in a room just off the kitchen on the first floor of the house.

Short on money, Mrs. Houghton ran a boardinghouse on the premises to make ends meet until her death in 1958. Mrs. Houghton did not die in the house. The Houghton children kept the house in the family until they were all elderly and could not take care of it anymore.

The exterior of the Stone Lion Inn. *Photograph by Heather Woodward.*

In 1986, Becky Luker bought the house and, with help of her sons, renovated it to become Guthrie's first bed-and-breakfast. The family lived up on the third floor. During renovations, Luker and her sons routinely heard footsteps and movement from the third floor and the back staircase. Luker went as far as calling the police on a few occasions, but nothing was ever found.

Doors would open and close by themselves. Luker's son would even prop things against a door to keep it open, only to have it slam shut.

The third floor, where Augusta (even though she did not die in the house) used to keep her toys, had the most activity. Luker's son used to put his toys away in the closet at night. In the morning, the closet was often found ransacked and torn apart, with toys strewn about the area. Though the little girl is hardly seen as an apparition at the Inn, her presence has been felt. She could be energy that messes with the items in the closet since that used to be her play area.

Between 2:00 and 3:00 a.m., guests of the inn have felt someone tucking them in at night or touching their faces to wake them up. When they come to, they realize that no one is actually there in the room with them. Others have complained that they heard kids playing all night and they could not get a good night's sleep. When they woke up, they realized no children were in the building. Children's footsteps can also be heard going up and down the stairways.

There is a man in the basement who emits the smell of smoking tobacco when he is around. He dons a top hat and an old-fashioned black suit. Many think he is F.E. Houghton pacing the length of the house. Sometimes, pipe smoke drifts through other parts the house, like Houghton is still checking on his family and making himself known.

Others have felt the presence of the man in the basement and believe it to be intimidating and overbearing. No one is sure if this energy belongs to Houghton or a different man from the time the house was a funeral home. The embalming table from the morgue is now sitting in the entryway of the inn. This could be why the man wanders the home if he is not Mr. Houghton.

A psychic who investigated the Stone Lion Inn around 2005 said the smoking man's name is Edward. He favored cigars and died of lung cancer. He lingers in the house because he does not want to go to the other side. He would rather live life in the home and mess with the female guests by playing with their hair and startling them.

She also said there was depressed woman named Sara on the premises and an older woman who functioned as a mother figure in the house. She stated that these ghosts came to the house during its funeral home days and that they were territorial of the house.

At around 4:00 a.m., guests have complained of hearing the disembodied voice of a laughing woman. Guests have been so frightened by the laugh that they have left in the early morning, never wanting to return.

AUTHOR'S EXPERIENCE AT THE STONE LION INN

Stephanie; my boyfriend, Buck; and I had a hard time finding the Stone Lion Inn. We were driving around in the dark around Christmastime looking for the giant house. It is not easy to find.

I figured it would be on a busy street or on a street corner, but the house is actually in a low-lit neighborhood. We drove by it two or three times before we realized it was the actual address we were looking for.

At first sight, the house is unassuming. It looks like an old, renovated Victorian-style house, which are popular in the Guthrie area. I was not impressed. We debated whether to go inside to take a look or talk to someone in the house. However, while tuning into the energy of the house, I felt like it was not a good idea.

There is something really off about the property. I imagine that at one time, it was probably a happy house with a lot of kids, a lot of mayhem and a lot of love. I feel like the Houghtons really loved the place. Then something went awry.

I am a very curious about the macabre, especially when it comes to anything supernatural. We were sitting in the car when Stephanie asked, "Do you want to go in?"

I scowled and said, "Naw."

She was surprised, too. She said that she did not want to go in either and that she wasn't sure why. We were all just kind of leery of the place.

Stephanie asked me to do a read of the inn. At the time, I did not know any history about the place. I had no idea about the ghosts. Full disclosure: I had heard about the little girl ghost but did not know the backstory about her; I just knew that the top floor had the energy of a child. Other than that, I went in blind.

During my first scan of the house, I searched for the energy of the little girl. Something about it felt off. It did not feel like a real ghost, more like a story that was repeated many times. So, there is a child-like energy, but it felt more like an egregore or a thought form looking for attention rather than a real entity. So, I pushed that energy aside.

Next, I saw a woman in the second-story window on the left-hand side of the building. She was an older woman in white with a bun on top of her head. She didn't give me a name, but she did seem stern, like a caretaker or a mother figure. Her white outfit seemed more like a reference to her being a ghost than what she was actually wearing. It seemed like an early 1900s kind of outfit, a Victorian-type shirt with a high neck and long skirt of a dark color. I saw her walking around the second floor and sometimes on the stairs. I did not see her leave that area. I felt like she was looking over the building or was protecting it from something. I am not sure what. She did not tell me.

I also saw a man in a Confederate uniform, but I wasn't sure if he was part of the house or was just a wandering spirit who showed up because he felt me scanning the area. He had dark hair and dark eyes, and he was proud of his outfit.

The top floors of the Stone Lion Inn are much more haunted than the lower floors. There is just more residual energy moving around there. I did get the sense that someone was disappointed about how the place turned out. They did not like the renovations or the fact it was a bed-and-breakfast. Maybe it was he energy of the Houghtons being sad that the house isn't in the family anymore.

Perhaps we did not want to go in because the house is protected by the spirits. Maybe it was just an off night. Maybe there was something else going on that we were not privy to that evening.

The thought form energy is interesting because the "ghost" that everyone thinks is Augusta is probably Irene. However, no one mentions the name Irene when they see children. It makes me think there is a thought form in the inn that has taken on the role of Augusta. It is not a new phenomenon. Many haunted houses have thought form–type ghosts. One of the most popular is "Zombie Boy" in the Oliver House in Middleborough, Massachusetts. The show *Kindred Spirits* has an episode that describes how a thought form ghost can be created. The premise is that the more energy you put into something, the more it becomes sentient, even if it never existed in the first place. Therefore, almost every haunted hotel has a lady in white or a cigar-smoking man or a child throwing a ball on the second floor. Why the second floor? Because that is where most EMF energy from electricity gathers. The lighting from the first floor is nestled into the ceiling, which connects to the second floor. Due to this, the even numbers of a location are always going to be more haunted, since it is theorized that EMF feeds psychic and ghost phenomenon.

If you are in the area, the inn is still worth a visit. If you go looking for Augusta, ask her if she is a thought form. Ask her what she is doing there. I bet you anything you will get some interesting answers.

11

NORTHEASTERN STATE UNIVERSITY SEMINARY HALL

600 NORTH GRAND AVENUE
TAHLEQUAH, OKLAHOMA 74464

Northeastern State University is the oldest higher learning institution in Oklahoma and west of the Mississippi River. It opened its doors as a Cherokee Nation female seminary in 1846. The original seminary was located in Park Hill just outside of Tahlequah, Oklahoma. On Easter Sunday 1887, a fire destroyed the building, and it was moved to the campus where it sits today.

In 1909, the university expanded into a school for training teachers called Northeastern State Normal School. By 1921, the curriculum had evolved into that of a four-year state college, and in the 1950s, the school started offering baccalaureate and five-year degrees.

Now, the university is a public school with satellite campuses in Muskogee and Broken Arrow. About 25 percent of its students identify as Native American. The school has majors in Native American linguistics, and Cherokee can be studied as a second language.

All the haunted activity on the campus is concentrated in the old women's seminary building. It also happens to be the oldest part of the school. There was so much activity in the building that the university used to offer lantern-lit ghost tours. People have reported experiencing weird sounds and odd smells while touring the building. Unsuspecting visitors have also spotted a woman in a black uniform and yet another woman in a white wedding dress.

The most notorious ghost of the seminary hall is that of Ms. Florence Wilson. She was the principal of the women's seminary for twenty-six years, from 1875 to 1901. Wilson lost her fiancé in the Civil War and dressed primarily in black as part of her mourning ritual. She never really got over the death and disregarded most men.

Her ghost guards the stairway to the dormitories, making sure men do not go up there. When they have gone up the stairs, men have complained of being nauseated or a feeling of uneasiness, like they aren't supposed to be there. Also, Wilson haunts her old accommodations, which are now offices for the staff. She does not like male staff members and will make them feel as uncomfortable as possible until they ask for a different office and move out.

Another common ghost at the university is that of a former janitor named Floyd, who supposedly fell down an elevator shaft while at work. It is said that he haunts the second and fifth floors of the seminary building. He is a mischievous ghost and likes to move around canned goods, knock things over and take posters off the wall. Students find him to be funny but also annoying at times, especially when he gets too lively.

AUTHOR'S EXPERIENCE AT NORTHEASTERN STATE

The Northeastern State campus is beautiful. It has sprawling green grass and cool architecture. There's a river that runs at the edge of the campus accompanied with wooden walking bridges and inlaid steppingstones. It makes the setting seem very quaint, like you just entered a mythical fairy world on the British Isles.

The seminary building has a cool Gothic feel, with its brick front, rounded towers and pointy roof. Just from staring at the exterior, it feels like it should be haunted. It is the apex of all legend and lore. It feels frightful and eerie. It needs a spooky soundtrack.

As of this writing, the entire front of the seminary's structure is being held up by horizontal rows of scaffolding. Areas of renovation are the peak environments for spectral and strange happenings. But is it just superstition and myth?

When I walked around the campus and its buildings, I didn't feel anything that made my hairs stand up on end or my spidery senses tingle. The whole place felt pleasant. I think a lot of the stories are probably real but exaggerated because of the old lantern-lit tour from the early 2000s. People started talking, and the ghost stories became more supernatural, like a spectacular game of paranormal telephone.

I was more intrigued by the remnants of an old building on the water's edge. The bricks of the building seemed blackened, like it had burned down in a fire. It felt old and had a feeling of trauma. I wondered what the history was around that burned cube in the grass, but there was not a lot of information.

My boyfriend, Buck, took it upon himself to talk to the employees in the seminary building. Since he lives down the street from the campus, he thought it would be a fun excursion, and he also likes to hound people for information.

He said the overall consensus is that the building is haunted, but nobody who currently works there has ever had anything profound happen to them. However, behind the seminary building, there is an older building that used to be part of the stables. Later, it was a locker room. Now, it is the financial aid building. The people he talked to said that building was definitely haunted, and nobody liked going over there. The place just felt creepy. Buck went back there to check it out and said he did not want to spend very much time in the building. He said it had an eerie feeling and that he did not want to be there.

So, if you are going to spend some time on the Northeastern University campus, check out the dilapidated, burned brick building on the edge of the water. Go into the financial building and take a peek. Do not be afraid to talk to the staff. They are nice and they know people go there looking for ghosts.

Go to the seminary building, too. Maybe it was an off day when I went. Ghosts are finicky. They show up when they want to, not when I need them for a book.

12

OVERHOLSER MANSION

405 NORTHWEST FIFTEENTH STREET
OKLAHOMA CITY, OKLAHOMA 73103

In 1901, Henry Overholser, also known as the "father of Oklahoma City," and his socialite wife, Anna, bought three parcels in the newly developed Classens Highland Park, just outside of Oklahoma City. Many of their wealthy friends wondered why they bought so much land in an area that was considered to be out in the middle of the country. The couple would be living on the outskirts of the social events they regularly attended and even hosted.

Overholser was a wealthy businessperson and the first president of the chamber of commerce in Oklahoma City. His work, social life and the train were all centered in the heart of the city, miles from where they were to create their home. However, the couple had a vision to build what is known as the first mansion in Oklahoma City.

The house was built in 1903 by architect W.S. Mathews in the Chateauesque style. The style features heavy ornamentation, steeply pitched roofs, spires and rounded towers that were popular details on sixteenth-century French chateaus. The French style borrows heavily from Italian Renaissance architecture. The mansion spanned 11,700 square feet and cost $38,000 to build. The carriage house was a separate building and added another 4,000 square feet to the property.

In 1905, Anna had her only child, a daughter named Henry Ione, in the mansion. In 1915, Mr. Overholser died in the house on the second floor. His wake took place in the front parlor. Overholser was so popular in the area that his funeral date was considered a holiday, and Oklahoma City closed so that people could visit the mansion and pay their respects properly.

Anna lived in the mansion until her death in 1940. Henry Ione became the heir of the residence, along with her husband, David J. Perry. Henry Ione died in 1959, and the ownership of the property was transferred to her husband.

Perry sold the property, including all its original rugs and furniture, to the American Institute of Architects and Historical Preservation Inc. Later, the mansion was donated to the State of Oklahoma and managed by the Oklahoma Historical Society. From 2003 to the present day, the residence has been the restored and maintained by Preservation Oklahoma.

People have seen the curtains on the third floor of the mansion open and close by themselves. It is said that it could be Anna fidgeting with the curtains, waiting for Henry to come home from work. It is something she would often do.

Employees of the mansion say that the third floor is always the most active. They have seen the impressions of someone lying in the bed when there is no one in the house. Things move around and go missing. There is a presence of someone even though no one is around.

The ghost most often seen in the Overholser mansion is that of a woman in white wearing Victorian-era clothing and the typical Gibson girl hairstyle. She has been seen meandering the second and third floors and walking down the staircase. People have encountered odd noises throughout the house, and the smell of roses comes from nowhere. Anna's favorite flowers were roses. During tours, people have had their hair pulled and have felt like they had been pushed.

PART III

CREEPY CRYPTIDS

Southeastern Oklahoma is bigfoot country. It is the least-populated part of the state and has the largest number of wooded areas. The area is home to the Arbuckle and Ouachita Mountains, plus five other mountain ranges. It also houses Lake Eufaula, which is the largest lake in Oklahoma by surface area.

It is a great place for a bigfoot to hide, since there are tons of remote wooded areas without many city dwellings. The woods are full of food, including deer, rabbits and coyotes, and water sources are abundant. Aside from the lakes, there are a plethora of creeks and rivers.

The most seen type of bigfoot in the area is the skunk ape. However, there are at least three known types in the woods. If bigfoot can hide successfully in the woods, it's plausible that there could be other cryptids hanging out there, too. We just have not discovered them yet.

The following are some of the coolest and most well-known cryptids Oklahoma has to offer.

13

BIGFOOT

SOUTHEAST OKLAHOMA

According to the website Satellite Internet, Oklahoma ranks in at no. 9 in bigfoot sightings across the United States. Though California and Oregon have more sightings overall, it is said that Oklahoma has more sightings per capita than anywhere else in the world. Legendary cryptozoologist Lyle Blackburn said he puts Oklahoma at the top of the list of habitats that are perfect for bigfoot. With its dense forests and large lakes, Oklahoma has the perfect geography to keep a cryptid like bigfoot hidden.

Most sightings occur in the southeastern part of state. Witnesses of bigfoot claim that he has thick, matted chestnut brown or black fur and a horrible stench. He is nicknamed "skunk ape" because you can smell him way before you can see him.

The cryptid ranges from six to nine feet tall with a heavy build and a wide girth. His footprints have been known to reach as long as twenty inches.

Every year, the City of Honobia holds a Bigfoot conference. On average, about five thousand people attend the weekend festivities, which include speakers, food, camping and helicopter rides. The small unincorporated community lies in a very remote part of east Oklahoma. Residents only started getting electricity in the area in 1952. The closest ATM is twenty miles away, and the nearest gas station is sixteen miles away. It is a heavily wooded area, and logging supplies much of the income in the area.

Bigfoot, also known as Skunk Ape. *Drawing by Rebecca Lindsey.*

Residents have heard funny sounds in the forest. One man said he heard rocks being crashed into the river by his house for a good forty minutes. His entire family was unnerved by the incident.

THE SIEGE OF HONOBIA

In 2000, a hunter named Tim Humphreys made a claim that he shot a bigfoot in his woods near his house. He stated that the cryptid had started stealing deer meat from one of his outside freezers. In a two-year period, it went from staying outside and eating what it could to tapping on windows and trying to turn the doorknobs of Humphreys's home. The hunter was so freaked out by the escalating encounters that he went after the beast. One night, he saw the creature outside going after the deer meat. He shined a light in the cryptid's face and shot him with a rifle from about seventy yards away.

As the massive ape-like monster retreated, he could hear the calls of other animals in the forest. The hunter said it sounded like there were more bigfoots in the forest and that they were talking to each other. He feared for his life and hoped the other creatures were not coming for revenge.

Humphreys waited until morning to see if the bigfoot was still alive. When he investigated the area, he said he saw blood spattered in the trees about nine feet up for about two hundred yards. He believed that two other bigfoots had picked up the one he had shot and taken it into the forest.

Later, a logger in the area told Humphreys he had seen something weird the night he allegedly shot the monster. He said he had seen two creatures carrying a limp third creature and that they were headed deep into the forest. The logger was so perplexed by what he saw that he turned his car around six times to try to find the cryptids to verify that he was not hallucinating.

The Bigfoot Field Researchers Organization investigated Humphreys's claims, but they did not find much. A rainstorm passed through the area, and all traces of the alleged blood were washed away. The researchers found a bloody deer in the woods near where Humphreys said he had shot the bigfoot, but no other evidence was found.

The townsfolk were not sure what to think of the story. Many believed him because they had their own experiences with the hairy beast. But a lot of people thought he was crazy and making up tall tales. It is said that Humphrey got so fed up with people making fun of him that he left the area. His wife did not care what people were saying as much as she was freaked out by the incident and didn't want to go back to the house.

If you want to venture to the remote woods and have your own bigfoot experience, go the Honobia Bigfoot Festival and talk to the locals. The Honobia Bigfoot Festival is held at the Kiamichi Christian Mission located on Highway 144 and Indian Trail Highway. If you would like to know more about the event, go to https://www.honobiabigfoot.com/.

14

THE GREEN HILL MONSTER

TALIHINA

The Greenhill Monster is said to be one of the first bigfoot-like creatures spotted in Southeast Oklahoma. It happened in 1971, when a group of high school kids decided to cruise through the backroads of Talihina after a pep rally to look for a place to party. The group pulled over into a wooded area and built a fire. One of the teenagers wandered off on his own to relieve his bladder.

The teenager said he felt something come up behind him and try to grab him. When he turned, he saw a monster with dark matted fur a few feet taller. He ran back to where his friends were and locked himself in a car. His friends had no idea what was going on.

Curious about why his friend had run off and hidden himself, another teenager took a flashlight with him to check out what was in the forest. He got distracted because he had to relieve his bladder as well. However, he kept the light in front him just in case there was something in the forest. About twenty feet in front him, he witnessed a giant, bipedal, hairy monster. Without zipping up his pants, the teenager immediately ran off and jumped into the vehicle with his friend.

By this time, the group of kids was wondering what was going on. The two teenagers told them what they had seen. Scared for their lives, they hopped in their cars and drove to a barn where they knew teachers and classmates were putting together a homecoming float.

When the kids told them about the weird bigfoot, no one believed them, but a teacher saw how freaked out the two teenagers looked. The first kid who had been attacked by the monster was still shaking and was as white as a sheet. The second kid was also shaken and still had not zipped up his pants.

Curious about the teenagers' claims, a bunch of teenagers and teachers got into their cars and followed the original group of kids back to the location where they had seen the creature. The county deputy saw a line of cars heading into the backroads of the town and thought something nefarious was about to go down. He called the sheriff to head out in the area to see what was going on.

The deputy and the sheriff showed up at the site and asked why everyone had congregated at the edge of the woods. They saw a group of teenagers with flashlights looking around. The two teenagers who had seen the hairy monster told the officials what they had seen.

Skeptical, the sheriff and deputy went into the woods. They came back a few minutes later, looking worried, and told the kids to stay away from the area. The teenagers wanted to know what they had seen. The officials did not say, but they were acting strangely and looked visibly shaken.

The next day, news broke of what had happened the night before. The creature in the woods claimed the name the "Green Hill Monster," and a group of teenagers went back to the area against the wishes of the deputy and sheriff. They hoped that in the daylight, they could find the thing that had visibly freaked out the officials the night before. While walking in the woods, the teenagers came across three dead deer. Their necks were broken, and they had been eviscerated. There were no bullet holes anywhere on their bodies. Whatever had gotten to the deer had picked them up, broken their necks and eaten their entrails. From that point onward, people in the area were leery of going into the woods alone at night.

Before the popular documented sighting, in 1970, a man named Dusty Road encountered a very tall, heavyset, upright-walking beast while hunting in the Talihina woods. Startled, he waited for the creature to leave and then fled as fast as he could. Shortly after the sighting, a herd of cattle was found mutilated on a ranch in the same area. Could this have been the same monster?

BIGFOOT HUNTING SEASON IN OKLAHOMA

In May 2021, state representative J.J. Humphrey announced that a new bigfoot documentary would be filmed in Oklahoma. He said the crew would mostly be filming in Oklahoma City and Honobia.

Earlier in the year, he filed a shell bill to create an official hunting season for bigfoot. Under House Bill 1648, the Oklahoma Wildlife Conversation Committee would draft up licensing permits, fees, dates and rules for the season.

Humphrey said, at present, there is a $3 million bounty to catch bigfoot alive. In order to receive the bounty, you must bring the cryptid in unharmed, alive and in a humane way. "We don't hunt bigfoot. Nobody wants to harm bigfoot. We're going to do a live, humane capture of Bigfoot," he said on the floor of the House of Representatives.

He extended the bounty to anyone from any state or country. He said that everyone had an open invitation to catch bigfoot in Oklahoma. "We're extending this beyond just our region and throughout the state. We are wanting the whole world to come to southeastern Oklahoma, to the state of Oklahoma, and get involved in our bounty—Oklahoma bounty, bigfoot bounty. So, we're excited to invite the whole world to come and participate."

15

THE DEER WOMAN
(THE DEER LADY)

One part fertility goddess and one part vigilante, the Deer Woman has a most curious backstory. She will aid you with your problems or seduce you and kill you, depending on who you are and how much she likes you.

The Deer Woman originates from the Woodlands and Central Plain tribes in Oklahoma. However, her story reaches out as far as the woods of the Pacific Northwest. She is neither a goddess nor a spirit, but she does travel between the boundaries of the physical plane and the netherworlds.

The Cherokee call her one of the *Nunnehi*, which means "the people that live everywhere," or the *Ani Yunwitsandsdi* which translates to "little men." She is considered one of the fairy spirits of Native American lore. They are an immortal race who help humanity. The Lakota call her *Taxti Wau*.

She is considered a trickster energy, on par with the fae of Celtic traditions. She is sovereign in her nature and enigmatic in her ways. The Deer Woman answers to no one.

In her benign aspects, the Deer Woman comes to women when they need help with fertility or love matters. She is a shapeshifter and represents fertility and love. People swear they have seen her dancing at local pow wows dressed in black with a shawl covering her head.

However, the Deer Woman has a dark side. There are many depictions of how she became a ruthless vigilante, but the following is her most common origin story. She was brutally raped and left for dead in the woods. A doe lay down next to her so that she would not die alone.

The Deer Woman. *Drawing by Rebecca Lindsey.*

In her anger and sadness, the dying woman called out to the gods with her last breath. She pleaded with them to give her life so she could find her rapists and avenge her death. Her request was accepted, and the essence of the doe entered her body. She was reborn as the shapeshifting Deer Woman.

On top, her body is that of a beautiful woman, but her lower legs and feet are that of a deer.

In this new form, the Deer Woman finds cheaters or men who abuse the femininity or innocence of women. She will transform into the most beautiful woman with striking brown eyes. She lures the men into the woods and then stomps them to death with her deer hooves.

Women do not have to fear the Deer Woman. She is their ally and will always be there to guide them and help them when she is called upon. So, be careful in the Oklahoma woods if you are a cheating man. You may not come out alive.

THE DEER WOMAN OF MOHAWK PARK

Mohawk Park
6700 Mohawk Boulevard
Tulsa, Oklahoma 74115

Mohawk is one of the oldest park areas in Tulsa, Oklahoma. It is said that the Creek tribes used to gather in the area for pow wows and rituals. In her more passive form, the Deer Woman is said to have shown up at the Mohawk stomping rituals as a dark-haired, big-eyed woman. She would talk to a man and try to lure him into the woods before disappearing.

Mohawk Park is full of large, lush trees that have been around for centuries. In her siren form, the Deer Woman hides behind the tree trunks and shows herself to unsuspecting men. She summons them by transforming into a beautiful, topless woman with big doe eyes. The trees hide her hooves. When the man follows her into the forest, the Deer Woman stomps him to death, and he is never to be see again.

If you want to encounter the Deer Woman of Mohawk Park, stick the wooded areas, but make sure you are of good moral character. If not, your curiosity may kill you. If you are woman, you may ask for her help. Like all fae, she likes tokens of honor, so make sure to bring her something for tribute.

16

THE OKLAHOMA OCTOPUS

LAKE TENKILLER: EIGHT MILES NORTH OF GORE
ON HIGHWAY 100, VIAN, OKLAHOMA, 74962
LAKE THUNDERBIRD: 13101 ALAMEDA DRIVE,
NORMAN, OKLAHOMA, 73026
LAKE OOLOGAH: 8400 EAST HIGHWAY 88,
OOLOGAH, OKLAHOMA, 74053

The Oklahoma Octopus is a giant cephalopod that is said to be the size of a horse with reddish, leathery skin and long tentacles. The creature wraps itself around unsuspecting victims swimming in the lakes to drown them and presumably eat them. Those who have gotten away to live to tell their terrifying tales show suction cup marks on their extremities where the cryptid tried to pull them in the murky depths of the lakes.

The Oklahoma Octopus is said to inhabit not one but three manufactured lakes in the Sooner State.

Aside from all the lakes being in the same state, there is nothing similar about them, except that they were all recently manufactured. They do not connect to each other, nor are they near each other. There is no clear reference point as to how all three of these lakes became associated with a mysterious giant cryptid octopus—except maybe word-of-mouth rumors and confusion about the lakes' names.

There are rumors of a Native American myth that includes a giant, red, leathery, tentacle-clad water creature that eats men alive. However, documentation is spare to nonexistent, and the legend primarily pertains to Lake Thunderbird.

Oklahoma Octopus. *Drawing by Rebecca Lindsey.*

THE LAKES

Built between the years 1947 and 1952, Tenkiller Ferry Lake or "Lake Tenkiller" is a reservoir just outside of Tahlequah, Oklahoma. The river was created by damming the Illinois River for the purposes of flood control and hydroelectric power generation.

The lake was named after the prominent Cherokee Tenkiller family, who owned the land where the lake was created. Tenkiller Lake is considered one of the best places to dive in the entire state. At its peak, the water can be at depths of at least 165 feet.

Named after the Native American legend about the supernatural bird of power, Lake Thunderbird is a reservoir located in Norman and was created as a source of drinking water. Built between 1962 and 1965, the lake was formed by an earth-fill embankment that spans 7,300 feet and is 144 feet high.

Due to its reddish silt and murky waters, Lake Thunderbird is affectionately known as "Lake Dirtybird" by the community. The lake has an unusually high number of drownings compared to other lakes in the area. Officials attribute it to drunk people slipping and falling into the large body of water.

Named after the Cherokee word for "dark cloud," Oologah Lake is a reservoir that was formed as a source of water for Tulsa and the surrounding cities. Its construction began in 1951 but was not completed until 1963; its facilities were not developed until 1974.

Actor and cowboy Will Rogers's family home, the Dog Iron Ranch, was relocated to the northeastern shores of the lake during the flooding and damming of the basin.

Oologah Lake is surrounded by horse country and has eighteen miles of horse trails.

THE LOST TAPES

The inception of the Oklahoma Octopus seems to stem from a 2009 episode of *The Lost Tapes*, a faux found footage cryptid-based show on Animal Planet.

The episode features a group of kids who are just graduating from high school. They jump into their convertible and drive to the local lake to swim since this is the last time they are hanging during the summer before everyone leaves for college.

Of course, one of the teenagers carries around a video camera the whole time, even in the water. While on shore, he catches a glimpse of something that looks like tentacles creeping up from the water's surface. He makes a note of it, but since no one else saw it, he brushes it off.

Another teenager steals a canoe, and the group of young adults hangs out on a platform in the middle of the lake for the rest of the day, talking about their prospective futures. The canoe-stealing kid is also a prankster and pretends that he is being pulled under the water by a large creature. Every time, he resurfaces, laughing and thinking he got something over on his friends. Nobody is amused.

Let us be clear: this is the most obvious and cringy trope of foreshadowing ever. You know how this is going to end, right?

Later, during twilight, the canoe thief tries to paddle back to the shore after he gets into a heated bit of banter with one of the girls in the group. Suddenly, large ominous tentacles reach out from the depths of the lake and suck the canoe into the water. The thief kid says he wants help and says something is pulling him underwater.

The teenagers think it's another practical joke, but he doesn't come up this time. Everyone freaks out. Two of the other teenagers try to find their friend and/or swim to shore, but they are sucked under by the giant octopus-looking creature.

By now, it is the middle of the night. The last two teenagers know they have to swim to the shore, or they will inevitably be eaten by the giant octopus that is lurking in the waters, just waiting for a human snack.

They jump off the raft and swim as fast as they can. There are screams and movement in the water before the footage cuts out.

At the end of the episode, it says that the last two teenagers were found on the shore, scared, exhausted and with blister-like marks all over their bodies.

Cue the foreboding music.

At present, there are no pictures or physical evidence of the Oklahoma Octopus.

AUTHOR'S EXPERIENCE AT THUNDERBIRD LAKE

My friend Stephanie lives about ten minutes away from Thunderbird Lake. She had lived in the area for most of her life. I asked her if she had ever seen anything strange at the lake. She said no. I inquired about the Oklahoma Octopus, and she had never heard of it. So, Stephanie; my boyfriend, Buck; and I went to do a little cryptid investigation to see if we could see anything in the area.

I have driven by Lake Tenkiller and Lake Thunderbird on a few occasions. They are both huge manufactured lakes and cover a lot of territory. It is easy to see how a story about a strange tentacled creature could start from a misinterpreted sighting of rippled water or perhaps even piece of a tree branch sticking out of water at just the right angle.

To add to the mythos, small squid and octopi have been seen sticking to the shallow part of the Lake Tenkiller Dam. Scientists believe these creatures are abandoned pets left by people who do not realize cephalopods can't survive in freshwater. Still, though, it does not take a lot of brain power to imagine that one of these smaller octopi survived the initial plunge into the lake water and learned to evolve and adapt. There is enough food and square footage in the lakes to handle something large and voluminous. Plus, it could hide well in the depths of the waters.

These were all things Stephanie, Buck and I considered while going to Lake Thunderbird. We went on a very cold evening during the holiday season. I remember the weather being in the low thirties, and there was a slight wind. I forgot to bring a jacket and had on a light sweater, but it did not deter me from see what the lake had to offer.

We went to two distinct parts of the lake. One part had beaches and shallow waters. Then we went to the deeper side of the lake, where there were boat launches. The sand on the beachy side of Lake Thunderbird was red and silty. There were park benches and areas for camping. Though, because of the cold, there weren't many people milling around. It was quiet, which was good for what we were trying to do.

The three of us walked down to edge of the water and stood in silence. We watched the water, hoping to see something that resembled a cryptid or anything that seemed weird. Not a lot happened. However, I did notice that when a light wind hits the water in such a way, it emits a loud, splashy kind of ripple. It sounded like something playing in the water. Even though I knew it was the wind playing tricks on me, I could not help but scan the area to make sure there wasn't something in the water that I missed. After sitting on the shore for a little while, the cold whipping through my light clothes was too much, and we headed over to the deeper side of the lake.

This time, we stayed in the car because the wind was heavier, and the overall energy of the place was more intense. We drove down the boat launch pad, trying to get as close to the water's edge as we could without risking our lives. The wind was whipping across the top of the lake, creating a cascade of waves. It was loud.

We sat in the car for a while, but nothing happened. After a good thirty minutes, we gave up. I'm sad to report that we didn't see anything unusual, but it wasn't for lack of trying. Is the Oklahoma Octopus real? I would like to think it is, just for my own amusement.

PART IV

MURDER AND MYSTERY

True crime is the most eerie part of Oklahoma history, because it involves real people with real lives. Their stories pull at our heartstrings because we can connect with their plights and empathize with the survivors. It's horrible to imagine that a child could go missing during the chaos of an F5 tornado disaster, but it actually happened. She was taken by two men who talked to nurses and employees in a busy hospital, never to return. The details of the case span decades, and it is said that over three hundred women came forward, claiming they were her.

There's a cold case in Lawton from the late 1990s that is still unsolved. Over a dozen women were dumped in bodies of water under bridges in five states. Over half of them were found near Lawton, Oklahoma. They had no exterior trauma, and most of their causes of death were undetermined or considered possible drug overdoses. The details of this case are unusual and mind-bending.

There are other cases that are mind-boggling and defy rational explanation. How were these killers never caught? How did authorities not take it more seriously? With the progression of DNA and modern science, should some of the cases have been solved by now?

These are all great questions. However, some cases just don't ever come together, and they leave an indelible print on our hearts and minds. The following are some of the most interesting and strangest true crime cases in Oklahoma history. Get out your murder board and your string and get the pot of coffee going—some of these are going to get you all fired up to catch a killer.

17

THE HANGING TREE

3 NORTH LAWTON AVENUE
TULSA, OKLAHOMA 74127

Sitting ominously on the grounds of the Oktoberfest headquarters is a two-hundred-year-old burr oak tree affectionately known as the "Creek Hanging Tree." Legend states that the tree was used to string up cattle rustlers and a handful of Creek tribe members between 1870 and 1889. The most notable hangings were those of three cattle rustlers who were executed at the same time.

Tulsa historian Dick Warner tracked the legend of the hanging tree to a man named Bill Bruner, who was known for exaggerating the truth and creating tall tales. However, with a six-foot-diameter trunk and the lowest branch of the tree spanning twelve feet wide, it is not a leap to think that the oak could was the perfect place for vigilante justice.

In the 1920s, during city development, workers who were installing a sewer line found three skeletons buried near the tree. This was enough to keep the tree intact, and homes and buildings were built around the oak.

In 1989, the parcel of land was proposed as the spot for a new criminal justice building. Locals created a petition to keep the tree, in fear that it might get torn down during the renovation. In the end, the Tulsans won, and the tree was able to stay.

Today, the Hanging Tree is in the National Registry of Historic Trees.

AUTHOR'S EXPERIENCE WITH THE HANGING TREE

Sometimes, you see something that seems simple and straightforward, but it holds the weight of the world on its shoulders. This is how I felt about the hanging tree when I saw it. Maybe it was the dark of night that made it so ominous, or maybe it felt this way because it was one of the last stops on the Tulsa Spirit Tour Bus Tour. But there is something off about the energy of the place.

The burr oak tree is larger than what you would expect. It sprawls out and canvases a large area. There used to be bench beneath it, where people could eat their lunches. Now, it sits in a parking lot, whispering its tales to the wind.

I am fairly certain the entire area is haunted. The tree felt like it carried a lot of deathly energy on its trunk. Sometimes, when I hear stories about the history of a place, I can tell it's made up. The heaviness is missing. The tension in the air is not there.

This place feels haunted. If you ever get a chance to go to Tulsa, make sure you see it.

18

JOAN GAY CROFT

This is one those weird cases that will get you going down a rabbit hole and haunt you because you want to know the truth, but nothing makes sense. How could a little girl go missing in plain sight?

On April 9, 1947, an F5 tornado tore through Woodward, Oklahoma, leaving the city in ruins. It struck without warning at 8:42 p.m., pushing through about one hundred city blocks and destroying over one thousand homes and businesses. Winds varied from 220 to 240 miles an hour and blew through the town, destroying it in five minutes. At least 107 people were killed, including three unidentified children and one girl who went missing.

That little girl was Joan Gay Croft. She had been home with her sister Geri and her parents the night of the tornado. Her mom, Cleta May Croft, usually worked nights as a telephone operator. However, the National Federation of Telephone Workers was on their third day on strike, which meant there were no connected telephones in the town. City officials had no way of being warned of the impending disaster.

The Croft house was toppled during the natural disaster. A neighbor went through the rubble, looking for survivors. Sadly, the little girl's mom had been crushed by a falling wall and killed instantly. Her father, Hutchinson "Olin" Croft, sustained severe in injuries, and her sister had minor injuries from the flying debris. Croft had a splinter in her leg the size of pencil but was otherwise in good condition.

The hospital in Woodward was overflowing with the wounded and severely injured. Croft's father was taken to a makeshift hospital that had

A drawing of Joan Gay Croft from the National Unidentified Missing Person's System (NaMus). *From the NaMus website.*

been set up at Baker Hotel. Croft and her sister were taken into the basement of the hospital, where those with minor injuries waited to be seen.

In a weird communication error, Croft's aunt Ruth got word that her two nieces were now orphans. Her brother's name had been listed as one of the deceased in the newspaper. Ruth went directly to the hospital to find the two little girls and take them home. However, once she got there, she found that her brother was alive and would recover. She discovered there had been another man named Olan Hutchinson (with an "a" instead of an "i" in his name) who had perished in the tornado. Relieved, she went to help with the clean-up and said she would return in the morning to check on the family.

However, Ruth came back to a perplexing scenario. She went down to the basement to check on the two girls and found only Geri on her cot. Little Joan was nowhere to be found. When asked what happened, a tearful Geri told her aunt that two men in khaki uniforms went through the basement asking for Joan by name. Once they found her, they picked up her cot and moved her out of the hospital.

Geri said her sister had been crying that she did not want to go. She wanted to stay with her sister in the basement. The two men comforted the girl, saying she was not in danger and that no harm would come to her. They said they would be coming back for Geri, too, so the two girls could be together.

The nurses told Ruth that the men in khaki had said they were moving Joan to Oklahoma City Hospital. Because they were at capacity and people were constantly being shifted around, they didn't think twice about the men taking the little girl. The two men never came back for Geri.

Confused and worried, Ruth called around and found that her niece had never made it to the hospital—even stranger was that she was never expected for a transfer. Panicked, Ruth called other hospitals, the morgue and even an orphanage to see if she could find the missing girl.

Three children were found in the tornado debris, an eight-month-old baby, a little girl between ten and twelve years old and another girl between the ages of three and five. None of the bodies had been identified, and no one came forward looking for their lost children. Officials took pictures of the last little girl because she fit the description of Croft, and they showed them to her teachers, neighbors and family members. They all agreed the body was not that of Croft. It is believed the whereabouts of the eight-month-old baby's parents were found. However, they didn't come forward because they could not afford the burial. The state paid for the burial of the unidentified children.

The search for Croft spanned five states. Her father made posters and plastered them throughout the area. He went on radio shows talking about his daughter, hoping that someone had seen or could explain what had happened to her. He explained she had a bashful personality and did not like to talk to strangers. She would hide her face and let her parents talk for her. Family members said she had a speech impediment, so even if someone had found her, it would be hard to understand her and get her name.

THEORIES

Croft was considered to be well-mannered and strikingly beautiful. She had a head full of gorgeous blond hair, porcelain skin and cornflower blue eyes. Some have theorized that a woman named Georgia Tann took Croft because of her beauty. Tann stole babies and children from hospitals and orphanages and then sold them to wealthy families for an exorbitant fee. She mostly worked out of Tennessee but could have had set up satellite baby broker rings in the area.

Others think she may have been taken for a ransom that went south. Perhaps the men took the child thinking they would get money out of her father but did not account for her injury. If left untreated, the wood in her leg could have gone septic, and she could have passed away before they were able to enact their ransom plan.

Both scenarios seem unlikely, and there was no evidence to support them. No other children had been taken in the area, and Croft's father did not owe anyone any money. The Croft family was part of the middle class, but they were not rich. Olin was a successful sheep rancher. However, his house had just been demolished in the tornado, so he had little to offer.

Olin got married only three months after the death of his wife, which seemed odd, even for the period. There were rumors swirling that he had gotten rid of his daughter so he could be with his new woman without any outside ties. Geri was his stepdaughter, so he had no parental rights to her. Getting rid of Croft would give him a new beginning.

There are lot of holes in this theory, given that Croft's mother died in a natural disaster. It was not a planned event. Plus, her father spent most of the time after the disaster in the hospital recovering from his injuries. He did not have a lot of time to mastermind the kidnapping of his wounded daughter. Even though he got married quickly, he spent the rest of his life looking for his daughter. There is not a lot of reason to think he had anything to do with her disappearance.

Little Miss X

In June 1947, a little girl with blond hair and blue eyes was found savagely beaten in Weed, California. A homemaker found her dumped in a field of overgrown grass, left for dead. She was taken to the hospital and immediately put into intensive care.

The girl was named "Little Miss X" or "Baby X" during the ten days officials tried to identify her because she was in so much shock that she could not talk. Many speculated the girl could have been Croft because she matched her description, except she was much smaller in size.

It turned out that "Little Miss X" was two-year-old Mary Jane Meddlin. Her mom and her boyfriend left her in the field because they had two other children and decided they could not afford a third. They kept her brother and older sister and went to Oregon. The boyfriend confessed to physically dropping her off in California but denied beating her. Her parents were charged with assault and abandonment. They pleaded guilty to the charges and were sentenced to twenty years in prison. Meddlin went on to live with her biological father.

Will the Real Joan Gay Croft Please Stand Up?

Over the years, women have come forward claiming to be the lost little girl.

In 1994, a woman named Jean Smith was sure she was the little girl who had been stolen from the hospital basement. She said she never felt like she belonged to her parents and that she didn't resemble any of her relatives. Smith said she would have "flashbacks" of scenarios and situations with people that she felt she knew but had never met in real life.

In school, she had a tough time keeping up with the lessons and the other kids in her class. Teachers suspected that she was younger than her parents said she was and that there were problems in the household that were not being discussed.

Later in life, Smith went to therapy and was diagnosed with psychogenetic amnesia, which means something traumatic in her life kept her from remembering her past. She was referred to a psychiatrist, who put her into a regression therapy to try to unlock her memories. Smith recalled scenes of blood and screaming.

After many sessions, she started to believe that she was not raised by her real parents. She took her birth certificate, her baby photographs and her footprint to the police. It was determined that they were not pictures of her. Her birth story had been falsified.

Around the same time, Smith saw an episode of *Unsolved Mysteries* and immediately identified with the story of Croft. She contacted the Croft family to let them know she was their long-lost relative. Smith talked to members of the family and ended up having a conversation with Marvella Parks, who was a direct relative of Croft.

She said she had had over three hundred women come to her saying they were the blond-haired little girl. The relative needed more proof. Smith showed Parks the scar on her leg and other scars on her back from glass hitting her body. The wounds on her body were similar to the ones Croft had received in the tornado. Convinced the woman was her long lost relative, Parks offered up DNA to be tested against Smith. In the end, it was not a match.

In 1999, journalist Robert E. Lee wrote a series of articles about Croft's disappearance for the *Woodward County Journal*. He received an email from a woman who claimed to be the missing girl. She stated that both sides of the Croft family knew where she was all along and said she had spent most of her life living in Oklahoma City. The woman signed her name "Joan Gaye Croft," adding an extra "e" to the girl's middle name.

Lee wrote the woman back, asking for details. The woman sent him a reply asking to meet at Penn Square, where she would tell him everything. She said she knew what had happened to her. She stated she did not want any pictures taken. She said she had repressed a lot of memories because of the trauma of having her mother die and fall on top of her. She said she would be forthright with whatever information he needed.

Lee tried to reply to the woman to set up a time for the meeting, but his replies came back undeliverable. He never received another email from the woman again.

Over the years, more women have come forward, claiming to be Croft, but so far, no DNA test has matched her bloodline. Her relatives surmise that by this time, if she hasn't come forward, she is probably dead. We will never know what happened to the little girl with the blond hair and cornflower blue eyes.

19

THE GIGGLING GRANNY

At first glance, Nannie Doss looked like a typical middle-aged grandma. She had a plump, friendly face and loved spending time with her family and her grandchildren. Anyone who met her said she was a sweet, charming lady who was kind and smiled a lot. She had only one little bad habit that got her put into prison—she liked to kill people.

In 1905, Doss was born in Blue Mountain, Alabama. Her controlling and abusive father did not believe his children needed a formal education. So, they stayed home and worked on the family farm. At seven, the little girl sustained a head injury while riding a train to Alabama to visit relatives. The train stopped suddenly, and she hit her head on a metal bar. She suffered chronic headaches and blackouts from the injury.

By the time Doss was a teenager, she dreamed of a fairytale love life with the perfect husband. She desperately wanted to get away from her abusive father and the wear and tear of farm life. She read the "lonely hearts" columns in romance magazines, wishing she could meet her ideal mate and fall madly in love.

At sixteen, she married Charley Braggs, who had only courted her for four months. From 1921 to 1927, the couple had four children. They lived with Braggs's mother, who was temperamental and abusive. With the stress of her mother-in-law creating rifts, the marriage started to fall apart.

The couple divorced in 1928, and Braggs took his oldest daughter, Melvina, with him. Two of the middle children had died under mysterious circumstances. They were healthy, lively children, and then they became

A photograph of Nannie
Doss. *From Wikitree.*

sick from food poisoning and died quickly. Braggs left his wife with their only
other living child, an infant named Florine. Braggs said he left Doss because
he was afraid of her.

A year later, Doss married Frank Harrelsen, an abusive alcoholic from
Jacksonville, Florida. The couple met through a lonely hearts column in one
of those romance magazines Doss loved so much. Harrelsen wrote Doss
love letters, and she sent him sexy letters with risqué photographs. After they
were married, Doss found out Harrelsen had a criminal record for assault,
but she stayed with him anyway. They were married for sixteen years.

During this time, Melvina's children mysteriously died during visits with
their grandmother. Her newborn baby died when Melvina thought she
saw her mother stick a hat pin in the infant's brain. Melvina relayed the
information to a doctor, but there was not enough conclusive evidence to
show that that was the cause of the baby's death.

Months later, Melvina's two-year-old child died from asphyxiation while
in Doss's care. Doss received a $500 life insurance policy that she had taken
out on her grandson. Melvina suspected her mother had something to do
with the child's death.

In 1945, Doss put poison in her husband's moonshine. He died a few days
later, and people assumed he had died from food poisoning. Of course, Doss

had a life insurance policy on her husband, and she bought a house and a plot of land in Jacksonville, Florida, with the payout.

This time, the grandma joined a dating service called "Diamond Circle Club" and found her third husband within months. He was another alcoholic named Arlie Lanning. In 1952, his wife added poison to one of his meals. He died of a heart attack, and doctors attributed it to his heavy drinking. She had a life insurance policy on him and immediately collected on it.

In 1953, Doss found another suitor in the lonely hearts column. His name was Richard Morton, and he liked to cheat with other women. However, his wife did not find out about this for a while because she was distracted with another matter. Doss's mother came to live with her after breaking her hip. After three months of living with her daughter, Doss's mother was found dead under mysterious circumstances. Shortly after her mom died, Doss's sister came to visit and ended up with a mysterious affliction that caused her death.

In 1954, Doss's last victim was a Nazarene minister named Samuel Doss from Tulsa, Oklahoma. He did not drink, he wasn't abusive and he didn't cheat. However, he did not like his wife reading the romance magazines. He forbade her from reading anything or watching anything on the television that was not meant for educational purposes.

Within a couple of months, Samuel ended up in the hospital after Doss laced a prune cake with poison. He survived the attack and spent a month recovering in the hospital. When he came home, Doss poured him poison-laced coffee, and he died instantly.

Samuel's doctor became suspicious of his death, since he had such a good recovery. He asked for an autopsy, and the coroner found that the dead man's body was riddled with arsenic. It was clear that he had been murdered, and Nannie Doss was immediately arrested.

Doss confessed to killing four of her five husbands but denied she had anything to do with her relatives dying on her watch. With the confession, authorities were able to exhume all of the husbands, and they found arsenic or rat poison in each of their bodies. Later, when the attention on her intensified, Doss confessed to also killing her mother, her sister, her grandson and one of her mothers-in-law. In all, it is assumed she killed about twelve people but only confessed to killing eight.

Doss became known as the Giggling Granny because every time reporters asked her about killing her husbands, she started to laugh. She said she liked killing because of the head injury she had received when she was seven. It changed her pathology.

The Giggling Grandma's mug shot photograph. *From Wikimedia Commons.*

Most assumed she killed her husbands for the insurance money, but Doss said this was not true. She said she killed her spouses because they did not turn out to be her true love. She was looking for "Mr. Right," but they had problems. So when she got sick of their issues, she killed them.

Doss was tried for the death of her last husband in Tulsa, Oklahoma. On May 17, 1955, she pleaded guilty to murder and received a sentence of life in prison. The State of Oklahoma did not ask for the death penalty because she was a woman. She was never charged for any of the other killings.

In 1965, Doss died of leukemia in the hospital ward of Oklahoma State Penitentiary.

20

THE LAWTON SERIAL KILLER

Lawton is a small city along I-44, about seventy miles outside of Oklahoma City. The area is known for Cameron University and the Fort Sill Army Base. It has a population of about one hundred thousand people, and according to Google, it is one of the safest places to live in Oklahoma City—well, now it is.

In the past, the city was known only for its series of unsolved murders of sex workers.

The first murder occurred during the sweltering summer of 1999, just outside of Lawton. A woman name Jane Marie Chafton was found naked, floating in Sandy Bear Creek Water in Stephens County. Decomposition had destroyed any forensic evidence, but it was obvious she had been murdered. Chafton had to be identified through fingerprints and what was left of her tattoos.

Chafton was a sex worker and spent most of her time on Cache Road, an area strewn with cheap hotels, liquor stores and unsavory characters. Traces of cocaine were found in her body, so it was assumed she had a drug problem. Because of her low standing in society, not much precedence was given to her case, and it was assumed her death was a hazard of her profession.

In October, another sex worker, Cassandra Lee Ramsey, disappeared from Cache Road. People close to her were hoping she had gotten sober, cleaned up and gone home. However, five months later, her naked, decomposed body was found by a farmer, half buried in mud under a bridge in Jefferson

The sign outside Lawton, Oklahoma. It shows how close Cache is to Lawton. *From Shutterstock.*

County. She had been murdered, and traces of cocaine were found in her body as well. Both women had no external wounds or evidence of trauma on their bodies.

In June 2000, a deputy with the Comanche County Sheriff's Office did a routine check at Bethel Road. The area was known to be a dumping ground for meth lab paraphernalia. Instead, he found the body of twenty-one-year-old Mandy Ann Raite. Like the other women, she was found naked in small body of water with no external wounds.

Raite, a known drug addict and sex worker, was trying to get clean and off the streets. She wanted to be a good mom to her toddler and had planned to pursue a career as an artist. Raite's official cause of death was considered a cocaine drug overdose.

Police had not put together that the three women had similarities. Their bodies had been found in three different counties, and all were considered casualties of their sex work, drug use and bad decisions. Never at any point did officials think there was a serial killer targeting street women.

In February 2002, two neighbors of an agent of the Oklahoma State Bureau of Investigations (OSBI) found a naked body floating in a pond under an old bridge. They called him frantically since the dump site was less than a mile from their neighborhood. The body belonged to twenty-nine-year-old Janice Marie Buono, who had been missing since New Year's Eve of the same year. She was a mother of three but also had a drug addiction and worked as a sex worker to pay for her habit. Her body had no signs of trauma, and it was assumed she died of a drug overdose. Buono had been found only three miles away from where Raite had been found.

Finally, the media caught wind that there may be something more than drug overdoses happening. They connected the women and postulated that there may be a killer on the loose. However, because these women were sex workers, nobody took the killings seriously. Only two stories ran in the newspaper. The dead bodies of sex workers did not seem like an issue to most because they felt they deserved it with their "high-risk" lifestyle.

Despite the lack of media attention and the lackluster investigation style of officials, the killings continued.

On June 4, 2003, yet another naked corpse was found floating in a body of water. This time, a farmer discovered the body of Pamela Woodring under a bridge in Kiowa County. Woodring had just gotten out of jail and was trying to get her life together. She went to jail for drug use and prostitution. Like those of the other victims, her body had no outward signs of trauma, and it was assumed she had died of a drug overdose. Her cause of death is officially considered undetermined.

Two months later, on August 30, the body of seventeen-year-old Tanja Marie Hook was found in a ditch in McClain County. Her cause of death couldn't be determined because of her body's decomposition from exposure to the elements. In fact, her remains were not identified until 2008 through DNA because of the condition of her corpse.

Hook was not an experienced streetwalker like the other women. Sometimes, she would work on Cache Road to get money. Hook did frequent the same motels as the other sex workers and was known to hang out with the wrong crowd. According to her boyfriend at the time, she got into a black truck with an older white man and was never seen again.

Then suddenly, the murders stopped without any rhyme or reason. Before the police even had a chance to work the case, it had gone cold.

DID THE KILLER PRACTICE ON OTHER WOMEN?

There may have been more murders that were overlooked because these women worked in the seedy underbelly of Lawton. They were drug-addicted sex workers, selling their bodies for money and commiserating with the worst of humanity. In the eyes of the community, it was almost like they deserved it. So, not much effort was put into investigating their deaths, which may have been the downfall of this serial murder case.

Back in 1993, a nineteen-year-old woman named Barbara Berry went missing. She danced at a topless bar called Deluxe and sometimes worked the streets for extra cash to fund her drug habit. Over a year later, in November 1994, her body was found wrapped in plastic and stuffed in a box that was covered in a plaster-like material. Her body had no wounds, and there was no cause of death. Her body had been exposed to the elements for some time, and it didn't give officials a solid cause of death. In the box with her were two T-shirts, two nails and a rock.

Before Berry, in 1991, another dancer from Deluxe went missing. Nineteen-year-old Tena Priest was last seen leaving her apartment for work. Her boyfriend went looking for her after he had not heard from her all day. He said she had left with a man and never come back. Berry and Priest knew each other and danced together at Deluxe. But Priest stuck strictly to the club. She did not have a drug problem and never walked the streets.

Priest's sister reported her missing and tried to get officials to take her disappearance seriously. But because of the nature of her work, it was assumed she had run off with someone or fell into a life of drug addiction. Her body was never found.

Between 1999 and 2004, there were a handful of other drug-addicted sex workers on Cache Road whose bodies were dumped in the area. However, they were not found naked in water, and they had obvious causes of death. Some still believe they are connected because of the number of killings of sex workers that happened in such a short amount of time.

THEORIES AND SUSPECTS

After the killings stopped, in 2004, authorities got together in Oklahoma City and compared cases from Tennessee, Texas, Mississippi and Louisiana. They discovered there were at least twelve cases of missing sex workers who were dumped in similar ways across the five states. But the bulk of the killings occurred in the vicinity of Lawton, Oklahoma.

One theory suggests the killer was a trucker who drove I-44 and had a home base near Lawton. Most of the dumped bodies were found under bridges and near main roadways. Another theory suggests the killer was a member of the military and stationed at Fort Sill. The murders would have then stopped when the soldier left the military or was moved to another base. The last theory postulates that the person who was killing was jailed for another crime and therefore could no longer commit crimes.

THE I-40 KILLER

John Robert Williams was a trucker who was arrested for the murder of twenty-year-old sex worker Nikki Hill. His girlfriend, Rachel Cumberland, was charged as an accomplice to the murder. During his confessions, Williams said that he had killed over thirty truck stop sex workers and that his crimes spanned seven states, including Oklahoma.

In August 2003, Jennifer Hyman, an Oklahoma City truck stop sex worker, was found dumped under a bridge in the Tallahatchie River in Mississippi. Her body had been stripped naked, and it was evident that she had been strangled to death.

Initially, Williams and Cumberland were attached to the murder, and due to this case's similarities to the Lawton murders, they were questioned about them. However, due to a lack of evidence, the charges were later dismissed. Williams was questioned about the following murders of sex workers from Oklahoma:

- In 2003, twenty-year-old Samantha Renee Patrick was found strangled and partially clothed behind a grocery store in Yukon, Oklahoma.
- Forty-four-year-old Vicki Helen Anderson from Sayre, Oklahoma, was dumped partially naked on I-40 near Grey, Texas.
- Thirty-nine-year-old Sandra Richardson from Oklahoma City was found in Okfuskee County, Texas, just north of I-40.
- Forty-three-year-old Sandra Beard was dumped naked in a ditch off I-40 near Oklahoma City.
- In 2004, nineteen-year-old Casey Jo Pipestem from Oklahoma City was found naked in a creek in Grapevine, Texas.

Unfortunately, Williams and Cumberland could not be attached to any of these cases due to a lack of evidence. Though there are a lot of factors that could put him at the crime scene, including his own confessions.

Most of the killings he confessed to had occurred on or near I-40, which was his main highway when driving his truck. The women of the Lawton murders were all dumped near I-44, which is another main highway for truckers. However, I-40 and I-44 don't intersect (except at an overpass in Oklahoma City, which can't be accessed by foot), so unless Williams went off his main route because he was familiar with the area, it would seem unlikely that he would pick up sex workers on Cache Road when he had access to truck stop sex workers on his normal route.

Williams did like to brag about his killing sprees. It is likely that he knew of another trucker killer and took credit for his murders. He could have even used a similar dumping technique for his victims. However, at this point, it is all conjecture.

For as much talking as Williams did, he also did a lot of lying. So, the truth may never come to light.

THE CRACKHEAD KILLER

Between September 2002 and April 2003, Cory Morris murdered at least five women in his trailer in Phoenix, Arizona. He would lure the women into his home by offering to pay for sex. During sex, he would strangle them and then cover them up with blankets and leave them in his bedroom, where he slept with them for days until they decomposed.

His friends and family would complain about the stench in his trailer, and Morris would blame it on his body odor and the extreme desert heat. On April 12, 2003, his uncle didn't believe the smell theory and went looking in the trailer for the cause of the stench. He found the maggot-covered corpse of the missing woman Julie Castillo under a pile of blankets.

Morris's uncle immediately called the police, and four other murder victims were found in dumping sites near the trailer. During his confession, Morris said he liked to kill sex workers because it was easy and nobody went looking for them.

He stated all five of the sex workers had died of drug overdoses and that he did not know what to do with their bodies. So, he hid them and then dumped them. All five women did have high doses of drugs in their systems upon death. Later, when officials didn't believe him, he recanted the drug overdose story and told the truth. He was convicted and sentenced to death.

Oklahoma authorities went to Phoenix, Arizona, to interview Morris to see if he had started his killing spree in Lawton. Even though the cases were similar, the way he dumped the bodies and kept them until they decomposed did not match the way the Lawton women were dumped. In the end, he did not turn out to be the right killer.

WILL PLAYING CARDS SOLVE THE CASE?

In 2017, OSBI created a new project, hoping to get eyes on the six main victims of the Lawton murders. Their mug shots were put on playing cards that were distributed to inmates in Oklahoma prisons. The idea was to hopefully get prisoners talking about the case and maybe bring information forward that had never come to light.

OSBI said in same cases, there could be a reward for the new information, but they were hoping enough time had passed that inmates felt safe to start talking about key players and what had happened.

The cards were also distributed to department of corrections facilities, and all the proceeds collected were put toward making other sets of cards with information from other unsolved cases.

21

THE CAMP SCOTT
GIRL SCOUT MURDERS

This is one of the most gruesome and bizarre murder cases in the history of Oklahoma. Three girls at the Camp Scott Kiowa Girl Scouts Encampment were brutally murdered a few hundred yards from their camp counselors and seven other tents holding twenty-eight other girls.

Their bodies were found 150 yards from their tent, intentionally placed near a major walking trail so that they would be easily found within hours of their deaths. What ensued was an investigation that included the sheriff's department, the highway patrol, the Oklahoma State Bureau of Investigation (OSBI) and the FBI. Later, over four hundred citizens from the area would join what would become the largest fugitive hunt in Oklahoma history.

The details of this case are beyond strange. There are twists and turns that make it seem like a bad Investigation Discovery shock documentary, but it really happened. It is all true.

The following is an outline of the case from the day of the murders to the present day.

JUNE 12, 1977

Approximately 140 girls were shuttled into the Camp Scott Girl Scout Encampment for the first night of a two-week-long summer camp. The girls picked out their tents. There were four girls to a tent. Michelle Guse (nine), Doris Milner (ten) and Lorie Farmer (eight) were put in the same tent

Tent no. 8 at Camp Scott. *Drawing by Rebecca Lindsey.*

together. There was supposed to be one other girl in their tent, but she felt sick and decided not to go to the camp at the last minute. This may very well have saved her life.

Milner was a shy newcomer and one of the few Black girls at the Girl Scout camp. The day before, camp counselor Dorothy Morrison recalled seeing Milner in a crowd. Her mother was worried about her daughter going to camp all by herself. Morrison assured her mother that she would

From left to right: Doris Milner, Michelle Guse and Lori Farmer. *Public domain, collage by Heather Woodward.*

be okay. She stuck with Milner during the hour-long bus ride from Tulsa to Camp Scott and escorted her to tent 8 because it was close to the bathroom and the kitchen.

Inside, Milner met up with Farmer and Guse. The three girls became fast friends.

That night, the girls braved a storm with heavy rains and huddled together in their tent. The tents were twelve feet long by fourteen feet wide with burlap sides, wooden floors and four cots for sleeping.

JUNE 13, 1977

Approximately 1:30 a.m.

A counselor got up to investigate strange moaning noises but could not find where they were coming from and went back to bed.

Between 2:00 a.m.–4:00 a.m.

A landowner in the area said that at around 2:30 a.m., he heard "quite a bit" of traffic on one of the remote roads leading to the campsite.

At 3:00 a.m., a camper in tent 7 woke up because a light was shone into her face. Another camper heard a scream. Another heard someone scream, "Momma, Momma."

Yet another camper, Wilma Tenant, stated she woke up because she heard screams. She went to her counselor, who told her to not to worry about it and to go back to sleep.

Sometime in the two-hour window from 2:00 a.m. to 4:00 a.m., the three girls in tent 8 were hit with a blunt object by a perpetrator (there may have been more than one). Two of the girls may have been killed instantly. Milner was bound and gagged, taken into the woods and strangled.

Approximately 6:00 a.m.

While on her way to the showers, Kiowa Unit Camp Scott counselor Carla Wilhite found the bodies of the three girls about 150 yards from their tent by a tree near a well-traveled trail.

She immediately saw Doris Milner's savagely beaten, mostly naked body strewn on top of her sleeping bag and knew that something horrible had happened. The other two girls' bodies were tucked in their sleeping bags and zipped up.

Approximately 7:30 a.m.

Local law enforcement arrived on the scene.

Approximately 10:30 a.m.

The camp was evacuated. Nobody was told what was going on, and they were left to speculate why camp had lasted only one night. Charter buses drove the girls back to Tulsa and arrived around 2:15 p.m.

The camp was closed for the investigation but never reopened—even to this day.

JUNE 14, 1977

The wooden floor of the tent was airlifted to a crime lab because of the amount of blood left at the scene. Whoever committed the killings tried to clean up the blood with towels and the mattresses in the tent.

Tent no. 8 in the Kiowa unit at Camp Scott. *Public domain.*

JUNE 15, 1977

Mayes County DA Sid Wise officially announced his outrage at the press for publishing information about two footprints found at the scene. A size 9.5 tennis shoe print was found inside the tent, while a different sized footprint was found outside of the tent. There was speculation that two different people committed the rape and murder of the girls.

In addition to the footprint information, the press was informed of other evidence collected at the scene. Notably, there were three fingerprints left on the girls' bodies.

A flashlight was left in the sleeping bag of one of the girls, and there were remnants of duct tape and a cord left in the tent. The flashlight had a thumbprint smear on the lens.

Convicted rapist Gene Lerot Hart was thrown out as a possible suspect. He escaped Mayes County Jail four years prior to the murders but was still at large in the area. He had family who lived in Locust Grove.

Hart was put in jail for the rape of two pregnant women. He kidnapped them, beat them and raped them. He bound them, stuck rags in their mouths, gagged them with tape and then laid them down on the ground. He covered them with leaves and then left them for dead. Luckily, Hart's binding techniques were not good. One of the women got loose from her hand ties, untying the other woman, and both were able to escape to safety.

A man living in his car about seven miles from the camp was arrested and questioned about the murders. He had no affiliation to the crime and was released the same day.

Jack Schroff, a ranch owner down the road from the camp, had a bunch of items stolen from his cabin.

JUNE 16, 1977

Nicknamed the "Wonder Dogs" by the press, a set of three tracking dogs were flown in from Pennsylvania to scan the property. Two of the dogs were German shepherds named Harras and Dutch. The third dog was a German Rottweiler named Butz.

The dogs determined that the killer(s) went past the counselors' tent to get to the three girls' tent. A pair of glasses and a case were found.

Three camp counselors were interviewed. It was revealed that the glasses and the case belonged to one of the camp counselors. Also, a denim purse was stolen from a counselors' tent the night of the murders.

The police went to investigate the scene of the robbery and concluded that there might be a connection between the ranch house burglary and the missing camp counselors' items.

DA Sid Wise made an announcement to the press that even though the girls may have been sexually assaulted by an unidentified object, he did not believe that the killer was a "woman homosexual."

JUNE 17, 1977

An article in the *Tulsa Tribune* reported that Jack Schroff, the ranch owner who was burglarized, passed a lie detector test. The way the article was written led readers to believe that he was a person of interest. He received a barrage of harassing phone calls and death threats. Schroff was so traumatized by the negative attention that he had to admitted to the hospital.

A telephone hotline was set up by the police hoping the killer(s) would call in and confess to the crime.

SOMETIME BETWEEN JUNE 16–JUNE 18, 1977

Rumors swirled that a Cherokee medicine man had placed a curse on the tracking dogs.

Late in the day on June 18, the tracking dog Butz died from heat prostration.

JUNE 18, 1977

Sheriff Pete Weavers made an announcement that they had found a murder weapon. However, DA Sid Wise and the Oklahoma State Bureau of Investigations (OSBI) claimed they had no idea what Weavers was talking about and said they weren't sure where he had gotten his information from.

The tracking dogs led investigators to a series of ponds on Schroff's property. Later, the ponds were searched, but nothing was recovered.

JUNE 19, 1977

Confusion and miscommunication set the tone for the murder case.

The Wonder Dogs' owner told the press that they had recovered evidence that would break open the case soon.

DA Sid Wise announced to the press that they had no suspects and that Sheriff Weaver was incorrect when he said a murder weapon had been recovered.

The OSBI stated to the press they had three suspects in the case, and Sheriff Weaver said there was one suspect.

JUNE 20, 1977

DA Sid Wise reversed his statement from twenty-four hours earlier and told the press there was a mountain of evidence and a bunch of suspects.

In a weird twist of fate, the tracking dog Harras ran into heavy traffic and was struck by a car on his way home to Pennsylvania.

JUNE 21, 1977

Oklahoma governor David Boren offered up the National Guard to help with the murder investigation.

A lone camper identified only as "Mike" was announced as a new suspect in the case. He allegedly stole a hatchet and some supplies from Camp Garland, a nearby Boy Scout campsite.

JULY 22, 1977

DA Sid Wise announced to the public a media blackout because he felt the newspapers were creating a false narrative that there was in-fighting between the authorities.

The forensics team announced that only one of the three fingerprints found on the body were useable. The other two fingerprints were too smudged.

Two photographs were discovered. There was a discrepancy in the way the photographs were found. Some officials stated that the photographs were found near the girls' bodies.

Another official said that the tracking dogs led investigators to a cave about two miles from the campsite. In the cave, there were the two photographs, a flashlight battery and a pair of glasses that had been stolen from a counselor. On the wall of the cave was scrawled, "The killer was here. Bye, bye, fools. 77-6-27."

Upon further research, the cave story is a conglomeration of three different caves in which evidence was discovered. The first cave was discovered by squirrel hunters four days after the killings. This is where the sunglasses were found. Other items included masking tape similar to the tape found on the flashlight near the girls' bodies and the two photographs.

The second cave was two miles from Camp Scott. There, investigators found boot prints that matched the prints at the girls' tent and Schroff's ranch, where the burglary took place.

The third cave was one mile from the campsite and sat on Shcroff's property. It was not found until July 7, 1978. A prison inmate led authorities to the cave. This is where the saying was scrawled on the wall.

July 23, 1977

The two pictures were posted in a newspaper for identification.

Authorities announced the two photographs found were originally developed by Gene Leroy Hart at the Granite Reformatory, where he worked in a photography lab. He was officially charged for the killings of the three girls.

A man with Gene Leroy Hart's description was spotted near Camp Scott. A search of the area was conducted to find the person of interest.

June 24, 1977

Over two hundred officers and four hundred volunteers circled a four-square-mile area of Camp Scott to search for the person of interest. Many of the volunteers brought guns, even though they were asked specifically not to carry. Some of the volunteers were arrested for being drunk, and there were others who were arrested for being under the influence of marijuana.

The search covered six square miles of the Skunk Mountain area. Items picked up were put into a white bag for analysis. The items found included two men's jackets, a pair of jeans, a T-shirt with sweat stains, a bunch of soda cans and a few empty egg cartons.

Members of the American Indian Movement (AIM) attended the fugitive hunt to watch over volunteers because Gene Leroy Hart was Native American.

June 26, 1977

A bulk of the two hundred officers who were part of the fugitive hunt left the area.

June 25–June 27, 1977

Heat-seeking devices were used in the search for Gene Leroy Hart. However, due to the excessively hot weather, they had no success with it.

JUNE 28, 1977

Sheriff Weaver stated a $14,000 reward was being put together for anyone who could help solve the case. The reward was put together by the Girl Scouts and the Pryor and Tulsa Banks.

JUNE 29, 1977

Over forty FBI agents were put on the murder case to help with the investigation.

JUNE 30, 1977

Gene Leroy Hart's mother talked to the press and declared she was being repeatedly harassed. Furthermore, she said Sheriff Weaver had planted the photographs due to of the mounting pressure to have a suspect.

The FBI made a statement explaining that they had found evidence showing that Gene Leroy Hart was in the vicinity of the campsite.

JULY 1, 1977

Authorities officially left Camp Scott.

JULY 5, 1977

A man matching Gene Leroy Hart's description was spotted in the surrounding area. Tracking dogs were sent in to search the premises but quickly lost he scent.

JULY 6, 1977

The Oklahoma State medical examiner released the three girl's autopsies in a press conference. Many of the "facts" that were given to the press during the initial investigation proved to be wrong after the autopsies were conducted.

All three girls were hit with a blunt object. One girl was hit only once, one girl was hit six times and the last girl was hit three times. Farmer and Guse died from head trauma. Milner was strangled. Two of the girls were bound, one with a thin rope and the other with rope and tape.

All three girls were sexually assaulted. Two of the girls were raped, and one of the girls was sodomized. The specifics of who received which kind of sexual assault were never disclosed to the public.

Despite all of this, in a previous statement, the medical examiner had said that none of the girls were raped.

OSBI director Jeff Laird stated in the press conference that there were no fingerprints on the bodies of the girls. His exact words were, "What were thought to be fingerprints were not fingerprints." He didn't elaborate or saying anything else on the subject.

During the press conference, he also said something very strange about Gene Leroy Hart. "I would say with certainty Hart is guilty because I would not say with certainty that any person who has not yet been tried were guilty, but we do have a great deal of evidence in this case that points to his guilt."

JULY 11, 1977

A personality profile of the killer was drawn up by Dr. Robert R. Phillips for the Associated Press. He believed that the person who committed the killings was a sadistic psychopath with sexual perversion who would kill again. He could be triggered by rejection and go into a rage.

He surmised that the killer watched over the camp to ready himself for the murders because he came prepared. He was under control during the murders and tried to instill as much control as possible, even trying to clean up the crime scene. Something frightened him, and he left in a haste, leaving behind evidence.

JULY 14, 1977

The final amount of reward money raised was $15,000.

JULY 29, 1977

A security team at Camp Scott saw what they thought was person wandering around in the woods near the murder site. Investigators went to the woods to check out the sighting. When they got back to the camp director's house, they found a plastic bag with a wet pair of Doris Milner's socks and shoes in them. No one knew how the shoes got there, and no one in the neighborhood saw who dropped them off.

AUGUST 3, 1977

The *Tulsa World* printed an urgent plea for Gene Leroy Hart to surrender and turn himself in.

Oklahoma governor David Boren stated, "I will use the authority of the governor's office and will take any steps necessary to assure his security and a fair trial if he will give himself up."

SEPTEMBER 22, 1977

The parents of Lori Farmer and Doris Milner filed a $3 million lawsuit against the Magic Empire Girl Scout Council. They lost the case.

OCTOBER 1, 1977

A group of Pryor residents called Drug Awareness Inc. offered up a $5,000 reward for any information leading to the arrest of Gene Leroy Hart.

OCTOBER 10, 1977

Sheriff Weaver told the press that he was confident Gene Leroy Hart was still in the area and that they would apprehend him.

Suspect Gene Leroy Hart being escorted by OSBI. *Public domain.*

DECEMBER 30, 1977

A report from the Department of Public Safety and the OSBI showed that they had spent over $138,000 (equivalent to $617,619 today) on Gene Leroy Hart's fugitive hunt. The figures did not include the money spent by the National Guard or Mayes County.

APRIL 6, 1978

At 4:15 a.m., eight OSBI agents stormed Sam Pigeon's home, which was located about forty-five miles from Camp Scott. Gene Leroy Hart was in the house and was immediately arrested. He was taken directly to Oklahoma State Penitentiary in Macalester, Oklahoma.

It was discovered that AIM and the Cherokee had been hiding Gene Leroy Hart in different households because they felt Sheriff Weaver was using him as a scapegoat instead of trying to find the real killer(s).

March 19, 1979–May 30, 1979

The trial lasted nearly three months.

The prosecution argued that Gene Leroy Hart had stolen the glasses from the campsite and that hair fibers on the duct tape left in the tent matched his.

The defense argued that Hart had stolen the glasses from a prior rape victim, the one whose rape he had originally been tried and incarcerated for many years back before he had escaped from jail. They posited that Sheriff Weaver had planted the rest of the evidence to incriminate Hart.

During the preliminary trial, Barbara Day, the director of Camp Scott, testified that she was told by Michelle Hoffman, a senior Girl Scout, in April 1977 that Hoffman had found a note that warned there were going to be murders at the camp. The note was thrown away because it was considered a prank, and no one remembered its exact wording.

Dr. Neal Hoffman, a medical examiner, stated that the girls had died between 4:00 a.m. and 6:00 a.m., only a short while before they were found.

Some of the campers testified they had seen two men wandering around Camp Scott shortly before the murders. The men were wearing khaki clothes and were seen by the latrines.

During the trial, Dr. Neal Hoffman, the Tulsa County medical examiner, testified the three girls were most likely beaten with the head of a camp axe. He explained how all three were sexually assaulted but said that one of the girls was assaulted postmortem due to a lack of bleeding from her wounds.

During the trial, waitress Dean Boyd testified that she had seen a nervous man with blood on him come into the diner where she worked. The diner was about fifteen miles from Camp Scott. The man was later revealed to be William Stevens, a convicted rapist, who had been seen at the campsite around June 13.

According to Steven's friend Duane Peters, the rapist had confessed to the killings in October 1977.

On March 30, 1979, a jury of six men and six women deliberated for five minutes before producing a verdict of not guilty.

Hart was sent back to Oklahoma State Penitentiary to serve a 308-year prison term for his prison escape and other charges. He died of a heart attack while jogging on June 4, 1979.

APRIL 19, 1979

A newspaper article reported that Stevens denied involvement in the Girl Scout murders. He said that he had never heard of Camp Scott and that he had worked at a Seminole construction site the morning the bodies were discovered. Duane Peters had also been interviewed. Both were serving time at a Kansas prison for the rape, robbery and kidnapping of a schoolteacher.

In 1989, DNA tests were performed on semen samples found at the crime scene by two separate sources. Hart's bodily fluids matched three of the samples' five probes. But one in 7,700 Native Americans could match the crime scene samples, which made the tests inconclusive.

For comparison, if all five probes had been conclusive, one in three billion Native American could match.

MAY 19, 2002

A report came out citing a 2001 DNA test. A semen-stained pillowcase from the girls' tent was tested against a sample from Hart. The same pillowcase was tested by the FBI in 1989. Both tests were inconclusive.

The 2001 sample was too deteriorated for significant results. However, from that test, there was the discovery of a partial female DNA profile. The partial was not significant enough to be compared against the DNA of the three girls.

JUNE 25, 2008

More DNA testing was conducted. No results came back from the sperm analysis. However, female DNA was again extracted from the pillowcase stains. It could not be sufficiently ruled that the female DNA had come from one of the three girls.

In 2018, nearly $30,000 was raised for another battery of DNA testing, but the request did not go through because the DNA samples were too deteriorated.

As of today, this case is considered open but inactive.

CONCLUSION

Oklahoma has its charm, but it also has its rebels and secrets. Its nickname, the Sooner State, comes from poachers of unclaimed land. The Natives who call the state home are the descendants of those who were forced out their homeland and pushed into new lands to start over whether they liked it or not. Much of the state still believes it's unfair the Confederacy lost. Race tensions were the fuel for the Tulsa Massacre, which left a scar on the city for years to come. Still, the people who live there make the best of their home. It is a proud state with some controversial events in its past.

However, the extremes of the state bring about a rich folklore and an eccentric history that you cannot help but be intrigued by. There are always untold secrets that can be peeled back like the layers of an onion if you take the time to do your research. It is a lush breeding ground for the eerie, the unexplained and the macabre. Try not to get lured into the forest by the little people's mischievous music or accidentally get sucked into a green light that takes you to the netherworld. The spook light seems like a safer route since you can watch from your car unless you accidentally run into the Native American chief with no head. Who knows, he may feel it is time to upgrade and take yours.

You can stalk the forest for all the different amalgamations of bigfoot and hope you witness him without losing your life, or you can search the lakes for the enigmatic Oklahoma Octopus—hopefully without being sucked into the waters and becoming another drowning statistic. You can heed the call of the Deer Woman with her big doe eyes and hope you have not forgotten about any salacious deeds in your past. She may help you, or she may stomp you with her giant hooves. It all depends on what she decides at the time.

Let us not forget the strange mystery of John Wilkes Booth and his alleged traveling mummy. Though we may never truly know its present whereabouts or its identity, we can still make our own assumptions and create our own theories. It is such an interesting story that it's hard not to stay up at night thinking about whether Booth was killed in that barn or if he really had the gumption to escape the authorities and mastermind his own fake death. Or was he just a good actor?

There are other questions that remain as well. What happened the Joan Gay Hart? Will her body ever be found? Who were the men in khaki uniforms who took her? Who was the Lawton serial killer? Will DNA and forensics ever give us the answer? And what of those three little girls in the tent no. 8? Will they ever find out who killed them? Will their families ever have peace? These are things that time and technology will hopefully answer.

In the end, we are left with a lot more questions than answers, but that is what makes Oklahoma eerie.

BIBLIOGRAPHY

Websites

Armstrong, Catherine. "This Oklahoma Legend Will Send Chills Down Your Spine." Only in Your State. January 21, 2018. https://www. onlyinyourstate.com/oklahoma/crybaby-bridges-ok/.

Ashley. "The Sinister Story Behind this Popular Oklahoma Park Will Give You Chills." Only in Your State. November 25, 2021. https://www. onlyinyourstate.com/oklahoma/sinister-beaver-dunes-park-ok/.

———. "This Haunted Road Trip Will Lead You to the Scariest Places in Oklahoma." Only in Your State. October 5, 2021. https://www. onlyinyourstate.com/oklahoma/scary-places-road-trip-ok/.

Astonishing Legends. "Stikini." May 27, 2019. https://www. astonishinglegends.com/astonishing-legends/2019/5/27/stikini.

Atlas Obscura. "The Center of the Universe." https://www.atlasobscura. com/places/the-center-of-the-universe-tulsa-oklahoma.

———. "Dead Man's Crossing." https://www.atlasobscura.com/places/ dead-woman-s-crossing.

Britannica. "Trail of Tears." https://www.britannica.com/event/Trail-of-Tears.

Cherokee Nation. "Osiyo!" https://www.cherokee.org/.

Clements, Joe. "Shamans Portal of Beaver Dunes Park." Puzzle Box Horror. April 22, 2021. https://puzzleboxhorror.com/shamans-portal-of-beaver-dunes-park-oklahoma/.

Cliburn, Justin. "Lawton, OK Serial Killer Who May Have Victims in TX, TN, MS and LA." Reddit. 2014. https://www.reddit.com/r/UnresolvedMysteries/comments/2vtxfh/lawton_ok_serial_killer_who_may_have_victims_in/.

Cover, Galen. "The Love Visitors Says Tour Coordinator about the Ghosts of Oklahoma City's Overholser Mansion." KFOR. October 11, 2021. https://kfor.com/news/great-state/they-love-visitors-says-tour-coordinator-about-the-ghosts-at-oklahoma-citys-overholser-mansion/.

Dalton Daily Citizen. "Town Crier: Little People of the Cherokee." April 2, 2021. https://www.dailycitizen.news/news/lifestyles/town-crier-little-people-of-the-cherokee/article_982ce1c6-8e96-5a6b-872f-61ba0673b993.html.

Davis, Amanda. "Jennifer Gragg, Part One." Oklahoma Cold Cases. 2019–22. https://oklahomacoldcases.org/the-lawton-murders.

———. "Jennifer Gragg, Part Two." Oklahoma Cold Cases. 2019–22. https://oklahomacoldcases.org/part-two.

———. "Jennifer Gragg, Part Three." Oklahoma Cold Cases. 2019–22. https://oklahomacoldcases.org/part-three.

———. "Jennifer Gragg, Part Four." Oklahoma Cold Cases. 2019–22. https://oklahomacoldcases.org/part-four.

———. "Jennifer Gragg, Part Five." Oklahoma Cold Cases. 2019–22. https://oklahomacoldcases.org/part-five.

———. "Jennifer Gragg, Part Six." Oklahoma Cold Cases. 2019–22. https://oklahomacoldcases.org/part-six.

DeLong, William. "Nannie Doss Spent Decades Murdering Relatives and Husband." All Things Interesting. March 1, 2018. https://allthatsinteresting.com/nannie-doss-giggling-granny.

Doctor Fright. "Stikini Seminole Legend." November 2, 2021. https://doctorfright.blogspot.com/2015/03/stikini.html.

Dwyer, John. "Oklahoma Gold." johndwyer.com. https://www.johnjdwyer.com/oklahoma-gold.

Explore Joplin. "The Spook Light." http://www.joplinmo.org/575/The-Spook-Light.

FBI. "Retired FBI Agent Reflects on Tragic Day and How It Shaped the Bureau." April 15, 2020. https://www.fbi.gov/news/stories/25-years-after-oklahoma-city-bombing-041520.

Floyd, Chelsea. "Lawton Cold Case Murders Featured in Deck." KSWO. October 12, 2017. https://www.kswo.com/story/36586216/lawton-cold-case-murders-featured-in-card-deck/.

Fortean Slip. "The Greenhill Monster Encounter." http://theforteanslip. blogspot.com/2017/06/the-green-hill-monster-encounter.html.

Girl Scout Murders. http://www.girlscoutmurders.com/.

Great Seminole Nation of Oklahoma. http://sno-nsn.org.

Haunted Places. "Henry Overholser Mansion." https://www. hauntedplaces.org/item/henry-overholser-mansion/.

Haunted Rooms. "Stone Lion Inn, Guthrie, Oklahoma." https://www. hauntedrooms.com/oklahoma/haunted-places/haunted-hotels/stone-lion-inn-guthrie.

Hex House. "Hex House Is Inspired by a True Story from Tulsa's Dark Past." https://hexhouse.com/about/.

History. "Timothy McVeigh Convicted for the Oklahoma City Bombing." June 2, 2021. https://www.history.com/this-day-in-history/mcveigh-convicted-for-oklahoma-city-bombing.

James, Louise B. "Did John Wilkes Booth Commit Suicide in Enid." *Oklahoman,* January 16, 1984. https://www.oklahoman.com/ article/2054048/did-john-wilkes-booth-commit-suicide-in-enid.

Johnson, Scott A. "The Stone Lion Inn." Dread Central. October 14, 2007. https://www.dreadcentral.com/cold-spots/5078/the-stone-lion-inn/.

Jones, Verona. "Oklahoma's Taxti Wau (Deer Woman)." Coffee House Writers. May 31, 2021. https://coffeehousewriters.com/oklahomas-deer-woman/.

Klein, Christopher. "John Wilkes Booth Mummy that Toured America." History. January 4, 2019. jhttps://www.history.com/news/the-john-wilkes-booth-mummy-that-toured-america.

KOCO staff. "Lawmaker Invites World to Participate in Oklahoma's $3 Million Bigfoot Bounty." KOCO. May 26, 2021. https://www.koco. com/article/lawmaker-invites-world-to-participate-in-oklahomas-dollar3-million-bigfoot-bounty/36547835.

Lost Tapes Community Wiki. "Oklahoma Octopus." https://the-lost-tapes-community.fandom.com/wiki/Oklahoma_Octopus.

Magaritoff, Marco. "Inside the Oklahoma Girl Scout Murders that Remain Unsolved to This Day." All Things Interesting. September 26, 2021. https://allthatsinteresting.com/oklahoma-girl-scout-murders.

McDonald, Megan. "One of the Most Haunted Bridges in Oklahoma, Boggy Creek Has Been Creepy Since 1924." Only in Your State. January 12, 2021. https://www.onlyinyourstate.com/oklahoma/haunted-bridge-in-oklahoma-ok/.

Meador, Granger. "Haunted Tahlequah. Meador." November 2, 2014. https://meador.org/2014/11/02/tahlequah/.

Michaels, Denver. "The Oklahoma Octopus." Denvermichaels.net. May 2, 2018. https://www.denvermichaels.net/the-oklahoma-octopus/.

Monroe, Heather. "The Twisted Disappearance of Joan Gay Croft." Medium. October 21, 2020. https://medium.com/lessons-from-history/the-twisted-disappearance-of-joan-gay-croft-3f87b443b32c.

Mooney, James. "The Little People." Over-Hill Indian Nation. http://www.fl-wolf-clan.org/littlepeople.htm.

Murphy, Jami. "Seminary Hall Haunted Tours Focus on NSU History." Cherokee Phoenix. October 18, 2012. https://www.cherokeephoenix.org/news/seminary-hall-haunted-tours-focus-on-nsu-history/article_b698e306-c6a1-5df3-af5e-ff5e17d6ee13.html.

Mysterious Facts. "Mystery Behind Center of the Universe in Downtown Tulsa, Oklahoma." https://mysteriousfacts.com/center-of-the-universe-circle-tulsa-oklahoma/.

National Parks Conservation Association. "Trail of Tears." https://www.npca.org/parks/trail-of-tears-national-historic-trail.

National Weather Service. "The Woodward Tornado of 9, April 1947." https://www.weather.gov/oun/events-19470409.

Norther State University. "Our Heritage." https://www.nsuok.edu/heritage/default.aspx.

Oklahoma City National Memorial and Museum. "The Survivor Tree—Today." https://memorialmuseum.com/experience/the-survivor-tree/the-survivor-tree-today/.

———. "A Symbol of Resilience." https://memorialmuseum.com/experience/the-survivor-tree/.

Oklahoma Historical Society. "Booth Legend." https://www.okhistory.org/publications/enc/entry.php?entry=BO016.

———. "Trail of Tears." https://www.okhistory.org/publications/enc/entry.php?entry=TR003#:~:text=The%20term%20%22Trail%20of%20Tears,Indian%20Territory%2C%20or%20present%20Oklahoma.

———. "Tulsa Race Massacre." https://www.okhistory.org/publications/enc/entry.php?entry=TU013.

Oklahoma Mysteries. "Unsolved: The Lawton Serial Killer." June 24, 2017. https://okmysteries.wordpress.com/2017/06/24/unsolved-the-lawton-serial-killer/.

OKPRI. "Stone Lion Inn." https://www.okpri.com/copy-of-basic-template-84.

Overholser Mansion. "History." https://www.overholsermansion.org/history.

Owen, Penny. "Dubious History Marks Bur Oak Tree in Tulsa." *Oklahoman*, March 24, 2002. https://www.oklahoman.com/article/2786822/dubious-history-marks-bur-oak-tree-in-tulsa.

Pursiful, Darrell J. "Yunwi Tsunsdi: Cherokee Little Folk." Into the Wonder. December 23, 2013. https://intothewonder.wordpress.com/2013/12/23/yunwi-tsunsdi-cherokee-little-folk/.

Route-66 Blog. "Crybaby Bridge." https://www.theroute-66.com/kellyville.html#crybaby.

Seek Ghosts. "Stone Lion Inn." August 1, 2019. https://seeksghosts.blogspot.com/2019/08/stone-lion-inn.html.

Severin, Kevin. "OK Ranks 9th in the Nation for Bigfoot Sightings." Fox 25. July 29, 2020. https://okcfox.com/news/local/ok-ranks-9th-in-nation-for-bigfoot-sightings.

Shea, Bex. "Monster of the Week Oklahoma Octopus." bexshea.com. July 13, 2016. http://bexshea.com/2016/07/13/monster-of-the-week-the-oklahoma-octopus/.

Shelton, Jacob. "Carol Ann Smith, the She Svengali, of Tulsa's Hex House Who Kept Two Women as Virtual Slaves." Ranker. November 22, 2019. https://www.ranker.com/list/carolann-smith-hex-house/jacob-shelton.

Southern Poverty Law Center. "10 Years Later, OKC Figure Walks Free." April 19, 2006. https://www.splcenter.org/fighting-hate/intelligence-report/2006/10-years-later-okc-bombing-figure-walks-free.

Stafford, Wayne. "Do You Believe? Film Crew on the Hunt for Bigfoot in Oklahoma." Fox 25. May 26, 2021. https://okcfox.com/news/local/do-you-believe-film-crew-on-the-hunt-for-bigfoot.

Team Ida. "The Urban Legend of Bigfoot in Oklahoma. Ida Red General Store." August 31, 2021. https://www.idaredgeneralstore.com/blogs/blog/the-urban-legend-of-bigfoot-in-oklahoma/.

Trammel, Robby. "DNA Tests Link Gene Leroy Hart to Girl Scout Murders." *Oklahoman*, October 25, 1989. https://www.oklahoman.com/article/2287953/dna-tests-link-gene-leroy-hart-to-girl-scout-deaths.

Travel Oklahoma. "Lake Tenkiller." https://www.travelok.com/listings/view.profile/id.4378.

———. "Lake Thunderbird State Park." https://www.travelok.com/state-parks/lake-thunderbird-state-park.

———. "Oklahoma's Spooky Legends." https://www.travelok.com/article_page/oklahomas-spooky-urban-legends.

Tulsa Historical Society and Museum. "The Attack on Greenwood." https://www.tulsahistory.org/exhibit/1921-tulsa-race-massacre/.

2 News Oklahoma. "How Was the Center of Universe Spot in Downton Tulsa Created." November 11, 2016. https://www.kjrh.com/news/local-news/how-was-the-center-of-the-universe-spot-in-downtown-tulsa-created.

Unsolved Mysteries Wiki. "James Gilwreath." https://unsolvedmysteries.fandom.com/wiki/James_Gilwreath.

———. "Joan Gay Croft." https://unsolvedmysteries.fandom.com/wiki/Joan_Gay_Croft.

what-when-how. "Overholser Mansion Oklahoma City Oklahoma (Haunted Place)." http://what-when-how.com/haunted-places/overholser-mansion-oklahoma-city-oklahoma-haunted-place/.

Wikipedia. "Abraham Lincoln." https://en.wikipedia.org/wiki/Abraham_Lincoln.

———. "Chateauesque." https://en.wikipedia.org/wiki/Ch%C3%A2teauesque.

———. "Cory Morris." https://en.wikipedia.org/wiki/Cory_Morris#:~:text=Cory%20Deonn%20Morris%20(born%20May,September%202002%20to%20April%202003.

———. "Dead Woman's Crossing." https://en.wikipedia.org/wiki/Dead_Women_Crossing,_Oklahoma.

———. "History of Oklahoma." https://en.wikipedia.org/wiki/History_of_Oklahoma.

———. "Honobia Oklahoma." https://en.wikipedia.org/wiki/Honobia,_Oklahoma.

———. "John Wilkes Booth." https://en.wikipedia.org/wiki/John_Wilkes_Booth.

———. "Lake Thunderbird." https://en.wikipedia.org/wiki/Lake_Thunderbird.

———. "Nannie Doss." https://en.wikipedia.org/wiki/Nannie_Doss.

———. "Northern State University." https://en.wikipedia.org/wiki/Northeastern_State_University.

———. "Oklahoma Girl Scout Murders." https://en.wikipedia.org/wiki/Oklahoma_Girl_Scout_murders.

———. "Seminole." https://en.wikipedia.org/wiki/Seminole.

———. "Sooners." https://en.wikipedia.org/wiki/Sooners.

———. "The Spook Light." https://en.wikipedia.org/wiki/The_Spooklight.

———. "Terry Nichols." https://en.wikipedia.org/wiki/Terry_Nichols.

———. "Trail of Tears." https://en.wikipedia.org/wiki/Trail_of_Tears.

———. "Tulsa Race Massacre." https://en.wikipedia.org/wiki/Tulsa_race_massacre.

Woodstock, Kieth. "The Deer Woman." Pioneer Woman Museum. November 1, 2018. https://www.pioneerwomanmuseum.com/history/the-deer-woman.

Wurtz, Maureen. "Bigfoot Expert Says Creature Highly Likely Present in Oklahoma." News Channel 8. September 29, 2016. https://ktul.com/news/investigations/bigfoot-expert-says-creature-highly-likely-present-in-oklahoma.

XUGU4RSIK1A6. "Restless Oklahoma: Shaman's Portal." jeanmariebauhaus.com. April 10, 2018. https://jeanmariebauhaus.com/2018/04/10/restless-oklahoma-shamans-portal/.

Books

French, Teri. *Tulsa's Haunted Memories*. Charleston, SC: Arcadia Publishing, 2010.

Kelly, C.S. *The Camp Scott Murders*. N.p.: CreateSpace, 2014.

Video

Burgess, Bruce, dir. *Bigfootville*. London: Bluebook Films, 2002. https://www.imdb.com/title/tt0436116/?ref_=fn_al_tt_1.

Seagal, Douglas, dir. *The Lost Tapes*. Season 1, episode 5. "Oklahoma Octopus." Aired January 13, 2009, on Animal Planet. https://www.imdb.com/title/tt1355377/.

Wilkerson, Michael, dir. *Someone Cry for the Children*. Los Angeles, CA: Barrister Productions Inc., 1993. https://www.imdb.com/title/tt5912102/?ref_=fn_al_tt_1.

CONTRIBUTORS

STEPHANIE CARRELL

Stephanie is a nondualist, channeler, Reiki practitioner and holistic nutritionist. In the middle of a relationship crisis in her twenties and searching for answers, she stumbled into practices that facilitated a spiritual awakening that enlivened her dormant psychic abilities. This has led her down a winding path to discover her love for classical tantra and yoga. As a born leader, Stephanie finds passion in creating and restructuring community programs and doing what she can to assist the release of stored trauma we currently face. When she is not attempting to save the world in true Aquarian fashion, you can find her podcasting, dancing or cheering on the Oklahoma Sooners with her family. Find out more about her current projects at www.stephaniecarrell.com.

REBECCA LINDSEY

Rebecca's full name is Mary Rebecca Lindsey. She is thirty-three years old, was born in Claremore Indian Hospital in Oklahoma and grew up in Tahlequah. She went to college at Northeastern State University in Tahlequah and received her master's degree from the University of Tulsa. She is Cherokee and Choctaw. She has always drawn and been artistic. She has had pieces displayed in the Cherokee National Holiday art show. She primarily gives pieces away but has sold some at times. She works full time as a software engineer for the Department of Defense and as a server administrator.

She is best known for painting with acrylic mediums on Masonite or canvas. She used to paint on fabric and unique items like throw pillows. She often does larger pieces that are five feet by four feet on Masonite depicting landscape scenes. She also enjoys painting scenes from space, portraits and sci-fi, fantasy and pinup art pieces. Some of her best work, however, is done in pencil. She captures realism and detail better in pencil and charcoal pictures. She loves Frank Frazetta's art, and she loves really colorful scenes of nature, as well as animals.

She wishes, one day, that she can have a gallery to display all the art she creates. She would not care if she sold anything; she'd just give it away if someone strongly desired it.

BUCK MULLE

Buck Mulle studies ancient myths and legends, as well as the occult and metaphysical. He grew up in South Texas and served in the Unites States Navy after high school. He moved to Tahlequah, Oklahoma, in 2020 and resides there today.

ABOUT THE AUTHOR

Heather is the founder of the *NVus Alien* podcast, an award-winning psychic and an author.

She is an award-winning clairvoyant psychic, channeler and medium. At present, she has done more than ten thousand readings and guided hundreds of clients with their most pressing issues. She is a certified life coach, certified crystal healing practitioner and certified Rose Priestess and works with the Magdalene Rose lineage. Heather consistently works with my Pleiadean guides, the Blue Rays and the Ascended Masters in the Sisterhood of the Rose. She specializes in multidimensional life path work, Akashic Records readings, past life integrations and twin flame or karmic relationships. For more information, go to www.nvusalien.com.

Visit us at
www.historypress.com